SPAIN AND PORTUGAL IN 22 DAYS

A STEP-BY-STEP GUIDE AND TRAVEL ITINERARY

BY RICK STEVES
AND MICHAEL MULLER,
CORNELIA STAUCH &
WOLFGANG ABEL

Published by
John Muir Publications
Santa Fe, New Mexico

Maps Jim Wood
Cover Jennifer Dewey
Design/Production Mary Shapiro
Typography Casa Sin Nombre

ISBN 0–912528–51–6

CONTENTS

Spain and Portugal in 22 Days

HOW TO USE THIS BOOK

This book is the tour guide in your pocket. It lets you be the boss by giving you the best basic 22 days in Spain and Portugal and a suggested way to use each of those days most efficiently. It is for do-it-yourselfers—with or without a tour.

This *22 Day* series originated (and is still used) as the tour handbook for those who join Rick on his "Back Door Europe" Tours. Since most large organized tours work to keep their masses ignorant while visiting many of the same places we'll cover, this book is vital to anyone who hopes to maintain independence and flexibility while taking a typical big bus tour.

Realistically, most travelers are interested in the predictable biggies— Alhambra, Prado and flamenco. This tour covers those while mixing in a good dose of "back door intimacy" with Andalusian hilltowns, forgotten Algarve fishing villages and desolate La Mancha windmills.

While the trip is designed as a car tour, it also makes a great three-week train/bus trip. Each day's journey is adapted for train and bus travel with explanations, options and appropriate schedules included.

The trip starts and ends in Madrid, but you may consider flying into Lisbon and out of Madrid (or vice versa). This "open-jaws" flight plan costs no more than flying in and out of the same city (get specifics from your travel agent). To adjust your itinerary for this plan, you'd probably skip a few cities in the north and visit others as side trips from Madrid and Lisbon. The savings in driving time you get from an open-jaws route gives you more time for some of the post-tour options.

A three-week car rental (split two ways) or a three-week first class Eurailpass costs $330 at this writing. It costs $600–$800 to fly roundtrip to Madrid. For room and board figure $20 a day for 22 days, totally $440. This is a feasible budget if you know the tricks—see *Europe Through the Back Door*. Add $200 or $300 fun money and you've got yourself a great Iberian adventure for $1,800. Do it!

Of course, connect-the-dots travel isn't perfect, just as color-by-numbers ain't good art. But this book is your friendly fisherman, your Spaniard in a jam, your handbook. It's your well-thought-out and tested itinerary. We've done it on our own and with groups. Use it, take advantage of it, but don't let it rule you. Try to travel outside of peak season, anytime but June 20 through August 20, so finding hotels won't be a problem; wear a moneybelt; use local tourist information centers; and don't be an "Ugly American."

This book should be read through completely before your trip, and then used as a rack to hang more ideas on. As you study and travel and plan and talk to people you'll fill it with notes. It's your tool. The book is completely modular and is adaptable to any Iberian trip. You'll find 22 units—or days—each built with the same sections:

1. **Introductory overview** of the day.
2. An hour-by-hour **Suggested Schedule** that we recommend for each day.
3. List of the most important **Sightseeing Highlights** (rated: ▲▲▲Don't miss; ▲▲Try hard to see; ▲Worthwhile if you can make it).

4. **Transportation** plan for drivers, plus an adapted plan with schedules for train and bus travelers.
5. **Food** and **Accommodations**: How and where to find the best budget places, including addresses, phone numbers, and our favorites.
6. **Helpful Hints** on orientation, shopping, transportation, day-to-day chores.
7. An easy-to-read **map** locating all recommended places.
8. **Itinerary Options** for those with more or less than the suggested time, or with particular interests. This itinerary is *rubbery*.

At the back of the book, we've included some post-tour options if you have more time. There's also a thumbnail sketch of Spanish and Portuguese culture, history, art, food and language, as well as lists of festivals, foreign phrases and other helpful information.

Efficient Travelers Think Ahead
This itinerary assumes you are a well-organized traveler who lays departure groundwork upon arrival, reads a day ahead in the itinerary book, keeps a list of all the things that should be taken care of, and wards off problems whenever possible before they happen.

This itinerary also assumes that if you were always that well-organized, you'd be President of IBM and wouldn't *need* a budget guidebook. Therefore, we've scheduled in some slack time to account for unanticipated problems. Do your best!

When to Go
Peak season (July and August) is most crowded, hot, and difficult. During this time it's best to arrive early and call hotels in advance (call from one hotel to the next; your receptionist can help you). Things like banking, laundry stops, good mail days and picnics should be anticipated and planned for. If you expect to travel smart, you will. If you insist on being confused, your trip will be a mess.

Prices
For simplicity, we've priced things throughout this book in dollars. These prices, as well as the hours, telephone numbers and so on, are accurate as of July, 1985. Things are always changing and I have tossed timidity out the window knowing you'll understand that this book, like any guidebook, starts growing old before it's even printed. Please don't expect Spain and Portugal to have stood entirely still since this book was written, and do what you can to call ahead or doublecheck hours and times when you arrive.

Scheduling
Your overall itinerary strategy is a fun challenge. Read through this book and note the problem days: Mondays, when most museums are closed, and Sundays when public transportation is meager. Saturdays are virtually weekdays. It's good to mix intense and relaxed periods. Every trip needs at least a few slack days.

Keeping Up With the News (If You Must)
To keep in touch with world and American news while traveling in Europe, we use the *International Herald Tribune* which comes out almost daily via satellite. Every Tuesday the European editions of *Time* and *Newsweek* hit the stands. They are full of articles of particular interest to European travelers. News in English is only available where there's enough demand—in big cities and tourist centers.

Recommended Guidebooks
This small book is your itinerary handbook. To really enjoy and appreciate these busy three weeks, you'll also need some directory-type guidebook information. Sure it hurts to spend $30 or $40 on extra guidebooks, but when you consider the improvements they will make in your $2000 vacation—not to mention the money they'll save you—*not* buying them would be perfectly "penny-wise and pound-foolish." Here is our recommended guidebook strategy.
General low-budget directory-type guidebook — You need one. The best we've found (if you can't read Michael, Cornelia, and Wolfgang's German editions), are *Let's Go: Spain, Portugal and Morocco* and the "Rough Guides" to Spain and Portugal. *Let's Go* is updated each year by Harvard students and is a spinoff of the wonderful *Let's Go: Europe* guidebook. Its approach is rather hip and youthful, and if you've got $25 a day for room and board you may be a little rich for some of its info but, especially if you're going to Morocco, it's the best info source around ($8.95, 528 pages, get the latest edition, ISBN—0–312–48188–8).

Mark Ellingham has written very practical guides to both Spain and Portugal. These are written for the British market (prices are in pounds and the guides are hard to find in the U.S.), but well worth chasing down. He has an excellent command of both cultures and a wealth of good info. (Spain ISBN 0–7100–9542–2, Portugal ISBN 0–7102–0345–4, each $7.95, not as fresh as *Let's Go* which is updated annually).

Older travelers like the style of Arthur Frommer's *Spain and Portugal on $20 a Day*, but neither it nor Fodor's is very practical.
Cultural and sightseeing guides—*Michelin's Green Guides* for Spain and Portugal are both great for info on the sights and culture (nothing on room and board). These are written with the driver in mind (on Michelin tires of course). The new American Express Guide to Spain (by Beazley, ISBN—0–85533–491–6, $8.95) is also great. The encyclopedic Blue Guides to Spain and Portugal are dry and scholastic but just right for some people.
Phrase book—*Berlitz Spanish Phrase Book*, $4.95.
Rick Steves' books—Finally, we've written this book assuming you've read or will read the latest edition of Rick Steves' book on the skills of budget travel, *Europe Through the Back Door.*

To keep this book small and pocket-sized, we've resisted the temptation to repeat the most applicable and important information already included in *Europe Through the Back Door*; there is no overlap.

Europe Through the Back Door gives you the basic skills, the foundation which makes this demanding 22-day plan possible. Chapters on: minimizing jet lag, packing light, driving or train travel, finding budget beds without reservations, changing money, theft and the tourist, hurdling the language barrier, health, travel photography, long-distance telephoning in Europe, travelers' toilet trauma, ugly-Americanism, laundry, and itinerary strategies and techniques that are so very important.

Rick's other book, *Europe 101*, gives you the story of Europe's people, history and art and would be a helpful preparation for this trip. Your bookstore should have these two books (available through John Muir Publications), or you can order directly (see page 104).

Books we would buy for this trip:
(1) *Let's Go: Spain and Portugal* (rip out appropriate chapters) $8.95, (2) *Berlitz Spanish Phrase Book*, $4.95, (3) *Michelin's Green Guides* for Spain and Portugal, $8.95 each. That comes to $32, or $16 each for two people.

Read *Europe Through the Back Door* and *Europe 101* at home before departing. Of all the books mentioned, only the Michelin guides are available in Europe; better yet, they are available in English and are cheaper there than in the USA.

Freedom
Our goal with this book is to free you, not chain you. Please defend your spontaneity like you would your mother, and use this book to avoid time- and money-wasting mistakes, to get more intimate with Iberia by traveling as a temporary local person, and as a point of departure from which to shape your best possible travel experience.

Be confident, enjoy the hills and the valleys, and *Bon Voyage.*

BACK DOOR TRAVEL PHILOSOPHY
AS TAUGHT IN
EUROPE THROUGH THE BACK DOOR

Travel is intensified living—maximum thrills per minute and one of the last great sources of legal adventure. In many ways, the less you spend the more you get.

Experiencing the real thing requires candid informality— going "Through the Back Door."

Affording travel is a matter of priorities. Many people who "can't afford a trip" could sell their cars and travel for two years.

You can travel anywhere in the world for $20 a day plus transportation costs. Money has little to do with enjoying your trip. In fact, spending more money builds a thicker wall between you and what you came to see.

A tight budget forces you to travel "close to the ground," meeting and communicating with the people, not relying on service with a purchased smile. Never sacrifice sleep, nutrition, safety or cleanliness in the name of budget. Simply enjoy the local-style alternatives to expensive hotels and restaurants.

Extroverts have more fun. If your trip is low on magic moments, kick yourself and start making things happen. Dignity and good travel don't mix.

If you don't enjoy a place, it's often because you don't know enough about it. Seek out the truth. Recognize tourist traps.

A culture is legitimized by its existence. Give a people the benefit of your open mind. Think of things as different but not better or worse.

Of course, travel, like the world, is a series of hills and valleys. Be fanatically positive and militantly optimistic.

Travel is addicting. It can make you a happier American, as well as a citizen of the world. Our Earth is home to five billion equally important people. That's wonderfully humbling.

Globetrotting destroys ethnocentricity and encourages the understanding and appreciation of various cultures. Travel changes people. Many travelers toss aside their "hometown blinders," assimilating the best points of different cultures into their own character.

The world is a cultural garden. We're working on the ultimate salad. Won't you join us?

Tour Route

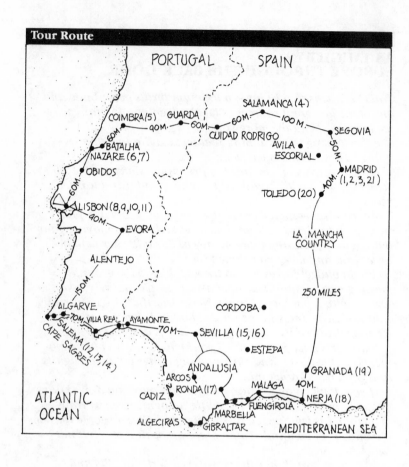

ITINERARY

DAY 1 Fly from the USA to Madrid

DAY 2 Arrive in Madrid, catch bus or taxi to Puerta del Sol to find your hotel. Get your bearings with an easy afternoon and evening. Possible stroll around old town.

DAY 3 Today we dive headlong into the grandeur of Spain's past, spending the morning at the lavish Royal Palace. After lunch and a siesta in the giant Retiro Park, we'll cover the canvas highlights of the Prado museum and Picasso's Guernica. Jet lag will lower its sleepy boom early this evening.

DAY 4 Spend the morning browsing through Madrid's old quarter and maybe the huge flea market. The afternoon is free for a bullfight, a side trip to El Escorial, or shopping. We'll spend the evening in the busy Malasana quarter dining late like Spain does. (This day is one of 3 easy-to-cut days on this itinerary).

DAY 5 We'll pick up our rental car first thing this morning (or catch the train) and head for historic Segovia where we'll have four hours to tour its impressive Roman aqueduct, cathedral, and Alcazar fortress. After a few hours on the road we'll set up in Salamanca in time to join the "paseo" (city stroll) and linger over dinner on Spain's greatest square, the Plaza Mayor.

DAY 6 Spend the morning exploring the old town and Salamanca's venerable university. Drive for about an hour for lunch in the walled frontier town of Ciudad Rodrigo and then cross into Portugal, driving through its wildly natural countryside to Coimbra in time to find a hotel and enjoy a dinner in the old quarter.

DAY 7 Spend the morning enjoying the historic center of what was the Portuguese capital when the Moors held Lisbon. After touring the university—Portugal's Oxford—have lunch and drive south for two hours to Batalha—the country's greatest church and a 600 year old symbol of its independence from Spain. The fishing village of São Martinho is nearby. Find a room and enjoy dinner on the Atlantic coast.

DAY 8 There's plenty to do during a circular morning excursion to small towns. After visiting a wine museum, an old windmill and the Alcobaca monastery we'll be ready for lunch in Nazare—a fishing village turned Coney Island. The afternoon and evening are free to explore Nazare, soak up some sun, take a swim, sample today's catch for dinner and watch the sun dive into the sea in Nazare or in our village homebase of São Martinho.

DAY 9 After breakfast we'll drive to Obidos—Portugal's medieval walled gem town—for a wander. Some of Portugal's most famous seafood is ours for lunch and we should be set up in Lisbon by 4:00. The salty Alfama quarter is a great place for an evening stroll and dinner.

DAY 10 This day in Lisbon is for relaxing, shopping and getting oriented. Spend the morning in the fashionable old Baixa and Chiado quarters shopping and people-watching. After lunch we'll enjoy the best view in town from the castelo and hike through the noisy nooks and cobbled crannies of the incredibly atmospheric Alfama sailors' district. We'll finish the day with drinking and droning in a gloomy Fado restaurant.

DAY 11 Now we get into Lisbon's history and art. The morning will be busy enjoying 2000 exciting years of art in the Gulbenkian Museum. After lunch we'll head out to the suburb of Belem for a good look at the wonders of Portugal's Golden Age—the huge Monument to the Discoveries, the Belem tower and the great Manueline-style church and cloisters.

DAY 12 Today we make a circular trip from Lisbon. First to Sintra with its hill-capping fairy-tale Pena Palace and the mysterious and desolate ruined Moorish castle. Then on to the wild and windy Capo da Roca. From this western-most point in Europe we go to the stately resort town of Cascais for dinner and an hour on the noble beachfront promenade.

DAY 13 Today we leave early for Evora, where we'll spend a few hours exploring and having lunch. The afternoon will be spent driving from remote village to village south through the vast Alentejo region. By dinnertime we should be set up in our Algarve hideaway—the tiny fishing village of Salema.

DAY 14 This is our "vacation from the vacation day," with beach time and fun in the Algarve sun.

DAY 15 A day to explore Portugal's south coast. After an elegant Pousada breakfast, we'll drive to Cape Sagres, Europe's "Land's End" and home of Henry the Navigator's famous navigation school. Spend the afternoon and evening in the jet-setty resort of Portimao or return to the peace and sleepy beauty of Salema.

DAY 16 Leave early driving across the entire Algarve with a few stops. By mid-afternoon you'll be on the tiny ferry, crossing the river to Spain where you're just two hours from Sevilla.

DAY 17 Today is for exciting Sevilla. After a busy morning in the Alcazar, Moorish garden, cathedral, climbing the Giralda Tower and exploring the old Jewish quarter, you'll need a peaceful lunch on the river and a siesta in the shady Maria Louisa Park. Spend the late afternoon browsing through the shopping district and visiting the Weeping Virgin altarpiece. Sevilla is Spain's late-night capital—get swallowed up in the ritual "paseo" and finish things off with dinner and a flamenco show in the Santa Cruz neighborhood.

DAY 18 We'll leave Sevilla early and arrive in Ronda late, filling this day with as much small town adventure as possible as we explore the "Ruta de Pueblos Blancos"—route of the white villages. The Andalusian interior is dotted with friendly and relatively un-touristed little white-washed towns.

DAY 19 After a morning to enjoy gorge-straddling Ronda's old town and bullring, we'll leave the rugged interior for the famous beach resorts of the Costa del Sol. We'll spend half a day on the coast not to enjoy the beach and sun as much as to experience a social phenomenon—the devastation of a beautiful coastline by sun-worshipping human beings. The headquarters you choose will depend on the atmosphere you want—hip, aristocratic, package-tour-tacky or quiet.

DAY 20 Escape very early to arrive in Granada by 9:00am. Spend most of the day in the great Moorish Alhambra palace with a picnic lunch in the royal Generalife gardens. Evenings are best exploring Spain's best old Moorish quarter, the Albaicin. This is a great place for dinner and an Alhambra view.

DAY 21 Drive all day to Toledo stopping for lunch in La Mancha, Don Quixote country. Get set up in the medieval depths of Toledo—Spain's best preserved and most historic city. An atmospheric (and delicious) roast suckling pig dinner is a great way to end the day.

DAY 22 Toledo has so much to see. Today we'll tour Spain's greatest cathedral and enjoy the greatest collections of El Greco paintings anywhere. Our tour ends tonight as we drive back to Madrid, turn in the car and check into the same hotel we stayed in when we began 22 days ago.

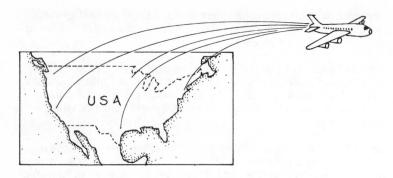

DAY 1
DEPART USA—MADRID

Call before going to the airport to affirm departure time as scheduled.
Bring something to do—a book, a journal, some handwork—and make
any waits and delays easy on yourself. Remember, no matter how long it
takes, flying to Europe is a very easy way to get there.

To minimize jet lag (body clock adjustment, stress):
■ Leave well rested. Pretend you are leaving a day earlier than you really
are. Plan accordingly and enjoy a peaceful last day.
■ Minimize stress during the flight by eating lightly, avoiding alcohol,
caffeine and sugar. Drink juice.
■ Sleep through the in-flight movie—or at least close your eyes and
fake it.

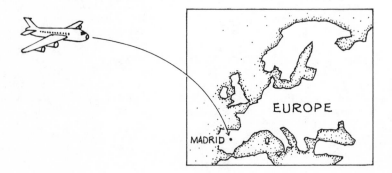

DAY 2

ARRIVE IN MADRID!

You always lose a day flying to Europe; if you leave on a Tuesday, when you land it will be Wednesday. Today will be spent getting acquainted with Madrid and finding a room for your three-night stay.

Suggested Schedule

Arrive at Madrid airport or train station.

Take bus to downtown.

Find hotel room.

Late dinner (in the Spanish tradition), relax.

Madrid's Barajas Airport is 10 miles east of downtown. Like most European airports, it has a bank that keeps long hours and offers fair exchange rates. There are also a tourist info desk, on-the-spot car rental agencies, and easy public transportation into town.

Car rental: If at all possible, don't drive in Madrid. Rent your car when you're ready to leave. Ideally, have that arranged through your travel agent at home. In Madrid try Europcar (García de Paredes 12) or Hertz (Gran Vía 80).

Airport taxis are notoriously expensive. Take the yellow bus into Madrid. It leaves about 4 times an hour for Plaza Colón.

If you're arriving by train from France or Barcelona, you'll dock at the modern Chamartin station. While you're at the station, make a reservation for your departure.

Orientation

Madrid is the hub of Spain. This modern capital of 4 million is young by European standards. Only 400 years ago, King Philip I decided to make it the capital of his empire. One hundred years ago Madrid had only 300,000 people, so while nine-tenths of the city is modern sprawl, the historical center can be covered easily on foot.

An east-west axis from the Royal Palace to the Prado Museum and Retiro Park cuts the historic center in half. The Puerta del Sol is dead center. In fact, this is even considered the center of Spain—notice the kilometer 0 marker at the police station from which all of Spain is surveyed.

North of the Puerta del Sol up to the Gran Vía is the old middle class quarter (18th century) with the Opera House and Royal Palace bordering this area on the west. North of the Gran Vía is the fascinating Malasana quarter with its colorful small houses, shoemaker's shops, milk vendors, bars, and cheap hotels. The Plaza Dos de Mayo hosts a lively scene each night. The Gran Vía, bubbling with business, expensive shops, and cinemas, leads down to the impressively modern Plaza de España.

To the south of the Puerta del Sol is an older district (16th century) with the great Plaza Mayor and plenty of relics from pre-industrial Spain. In the Lavapies quarter (southeast of Plaza Mayor) notice the names of the streets: Calles de Cuchilleros (knife smiths), Laterones (brass-casters), Bordaderos (embroiderers), Tinteros (dyers), Curtideros (tanners).

West of the Puerta del Sol is Madrid's huge museum (Prado), huge park (Retiro), and tiny river (Manzanares). Just north of the park is the elegant Salamanca quarter.

Accommodations
Madrid has plenty of centrally located budget hotels and pensions. Cabs are cheap. Upon arrival downtown, I'd take one to the Puerta del Sol and wander generally south and east. Doorbells line each building entrance. Push one that says "pension." You'll have no trouble finding a decent double for $12 to $20.

Choose small streets. The rooms get cheaper—and seedier—as you approach the Atocha station. Hotels on Gran Vía are more expensive and less atmospheric, but are still a good value.

Good central places with garages for those driving are Hostal Pereda (Valverde 1, tel. 222–4700) and Hostal Salas (Gran Vía 38, tel. 231–9699).

Our favorites right on the Puerta del Sol are "Marimart" (#14, tel. 222–9815) and "Sol" (#9).

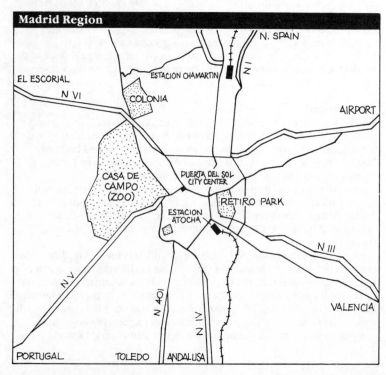

Madrid Region

Madrid has two good youth hostels—Santa Cruz de Marcenado (on Calle Santa Cruz de Marcenado 28, tel. 247–4532 near metro stop Arguelles, quite nice in a student neighborhood, cheap, 12:30 curfew), and youth hostel Richard Schirrman (Casa de Campo, tel. 463–5699, near metro El Lago, midnight curfew).

Food

Madrid loves to eat well and cheaply. Only Barcelona rivals Madrid in Spain for eating excitement. You have two basic dining choices: an atmospheric sit-down meal in a well-chosen restaurant or a potentially more atmospheric mobile meal doing the popular "tapa tango"—a local tradition of going from one bar to the next munching, drinking, and socializing.

Our favorite sit-down restaurants are : Zalacaín (Alvaraz de Baena 4, closed Sundays and all of August, with garden and terrace), El Amparo (Callejon de Puigcerda 8, closed Sundays and August), Jockey (Amador de los Rios 6, also closed Sundays and August). Also good are Sixto Gran Mesón (Cervantes 28, near Hotel Palace and the Prado), Casa Lucio (Cava Baja 35 in old town), El Schotis (Cava Baja II, closed Sunday and August), and Restaurante La Villa de Luarca (Concepción Arenal 6, just off Gran Via).

Most Americans are drawn to Hemingway's favorite, El Botín, (Cuchilleros 17 in old town). It's frighteningly touristy. Good vegetarian food is served at La Galette (Conda de Aranda 11, near Archeological museum). Your hotel receptionist is a reliable source for more info.

For tapa bars, try this route: from Puerta del Sol along Calles Victoria de la Cruz, Echegaray, del Pozo, and Nuñez del Arce.

Each night the Malasana quarter around the Plaza Dos de Mayo erupts with street life. This is Madrid's new bohemian, intellectual, liberal scene that has flowered only since the death of Franco. Artists, actors, former exiles, and Madrid's youth gather here. "Pepe Botella" is a fun restaurant, and tapa bars abound in this district. Try the old Café Gijón (Paseo de Recoletos 21), Comercial (Glorieta de Bilbao 10, north of Manuela Malasana) or Bocaccio.

After dinner, the best ice cream shops are at Calles Goya 68, Barcalo 1, Tirso de Molina 9, Magallanes 13, Lopez de Hoyos 106.

You'll find live music around Plaza Dos de Mayo and jazz at Whisky Jazz (Diego de León 7), Manuela (San Vicente Ferrer 29), and Ragtime (Ruiz 20). Flamenco is difficult to pin down since the "in places" change very fast. Try Arco de Cuchilleros (Cuchilleros 7, metro stop Sol), Las Brujas (Norte 15, metro San Bernardo, tel. 222–5325, 9:30–3:00am), Café de Chinitas (Torija 7), Café de la Morería (Moreria 17), or, better yet, ask your hotel receptionist.

On this first day in Madrid, you'll be set up by evening, enjoying a relaxing dinner and resting up for sightseeing the next day.

Helpful Hints

Madrid's subway—cheap and simple—is the pride of the Spanish public transportation system. Pick up a free map ("Plano del Metro") at any station. Runs from 6:00am to 1:30am.

City buses are not so cheap or easy but still good. Get info and schedules at the booth on Puerta del Sol.

Remember, if you're returning to Madrid at the end of your trip, make a reservation at the hotel of your choice. If you pay in advance, you can arrive as late as you like. You can also leave anything you won't need in the hotel's storage closet free (have your name and return date clearly indicated).

Because of the threat of terrorist bombs, you can no longer store luggage at the Madrid or Barcelona train stations. Don't worry, though. Local entrepreneurs have set up alternative baggage-checking facilities just a block or so away.

The main Tourist Information office is at Plaza Mayor 3 (M-F 10:00–1:30, 4:00–7:00, Sat. 10:00–1:30. tel. 266–5477), with other offices on Plaza España, in train stations and at the airport. Pick up a city map (free) and list of accomodations, confirm your sightseeing plans and hours, and use their handy English language monthly newsletter "En Madrid." "Guía del Ocio" is another good periodical entertainment guide (available at any kiosk).

U.S. Embassy: Serrano 75. Tel. (091) 276–3600 or, for emergencies, (091) 276–3229.

DAY 3

This is the day for the main sights of Madrid, visiting the Royal Palace and one of the world's great art museums—the Prado.

Suggested Schedule

9:00	Stroll around Puerta del Sol, through Plaza Mayor and to Palacio Real.
9:45	Be at the Palacio Real when it opens. Tour palace, armory, pharmacy, library.
1:00	Taxi to the Parque del Retiro. Have a bocadillo (sandwich) in a cafe.
2:00	Prado Museum. Save time and energy for Picasso's Guernica. (If you're too zombied by jet lag, do the Prado tomorrow morning).
6:00	Back to hotel for a rest. Most likely have a simple dinner and surrender to jet lag.

Sightseeing Highlights

▲▲▲**Prado Museum**—Our favorite art museum in Europe. Over 3,000 paintings, including rooms of masterpieces by Velazquez, Goya, El Greco, and Bosch. It's hot and overwhelming. Take a tour or buy a guidebook. Follow Goya through his cheery, political ("The Third of May") and dark stages ("Saturn Devouring His Children").

Goya, in all three of his "stages," asserted his independence from artistic conventions. Even the standard court portraits of his "first" stage reflect his politically liberal viewpoint, subtly showing the vanity and stupidity of his subjects by the look in their eyes. His political stage, with paintings like "The Third of May," depicting a massacre of Spaniards by Napoleon's troops, makes him one of the first artists with a social conscience. Finally, in his "dark stage," Goya probed the inner world of fears and nightmares, anticipating the 20th century preoccupation with dreams.

Also, don't miss El Bosco's ("Bosch" in Spanish) "Garden of Delights." Good cafeteria, great print and book shop. You can visit twice in one day with the same ticket. Open 10–6, Sunday 10–2, closed Mondays. It's free on Saturday, which maximizes crowd problems.

▲▲**Picasso's Guernica**—In the Casa de Buen Retiro, next to the Prado. This famous anti-war painting deserves much study. The death of Franco ended the work's American exile and now it reigns as Spain's national piece of art—behind bullet-proof glass. Your Prado ticket is good here, same hours as the Prado except Wednesday, 3–9.

▲▲**Royal Palace** (Palacio Real)—Europe's third greatest palace after Versailles and Vienna, and packed with tourists. Lavish interior. English tour included—and required. Open Mon—Sat, 10–12:45, 4–5:45, Sunday 10–12:45.

▲▲**El Rastro**—Europe's biggest flea market and a field day for people-watchers. Sunday from 9:00–1:00 (Now there's a smaller version on Fri. and Sat.). Thousands of stalls entertain over a million browsers. If you like garage sales, you'll love this. You can buy or sell nearly anything here. Start at the Plaza Mayor or take the subway to Tirso de Molina. Hang onto your wallet. Munch on a sweet Pepito or a relleno (sweet pudding-filled pastry). Europe's biggest stamp market thrives simultaneously on the Plaza Mayor.

▲▲**Malasana** quarter—Night scene and music near the Plaza Dos de Mayo.

▲**Chapell San Antonio de la Florida**—The grave of Goya under a cupola filled with Goya frescos. (M,T, Th, Sat 10–1, 4–7. Sun 10–1).

▲**Retiro Park**—350 acres of green breezy escape from the city. Rent a row boat, have a picnic. Peaceful gardens, great people-watching.

▲▲**Bullfight**—Madrid's "Plaza de Toros" (metro stop Ventas) hosts Spain's top bullfights nearly every Sunday and many Thursdays from Easter through October. Top fights sell out in advance but you can generally get a ticket at the door. Fights start at 5:00 or 7:00 and are one of the few examples of punctuality in Spain. There are no bad seats: paying more gets you in the shade and/or closer to the gore.

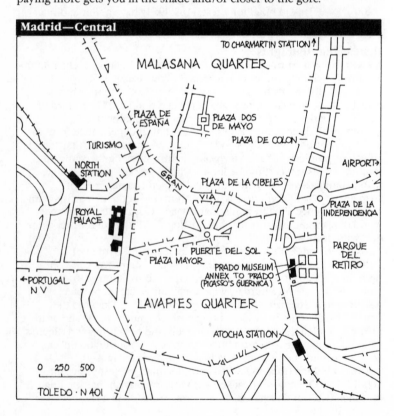

Madrid—Central

DAY 4
MADRID AND SIDE TRIPS

Today allows you time to soak in some of Madrid's colorful, cosmopolitan atmosphere, return to the Prado, or take a side trip.

Suggested Schedule	
9:00	Explore El Rastro flea market (F, S, or Sun) or just browse through old quarter south of Puerta del Sol.
11:00	Chapell San Antonio de la Florida.
1:00	Afternoon free for side trip, siesta, or bullfight (most Sundays, some Thursdays).
8:00	Stroll around the Malasana quarter. Find dinner.

Side Trips from Madrid
El Escorial 25 miles northwest of Madrid.— A symbol of power rather than elegance, this 16th century palace gives us a better feel for the Inquisition than any other building. Its construction dominated the Spanish economy for 20 years. For that reason Madrid has almost nothing else to show from this most powerful period of Spanish history. This giant gloomy building (grey-black stone, 2500 windows, 200 x 150 yards) looks more like a prison than a palace. 400 years ago Philip II ruled his bulky empire and directed the Inquisition from here. It's full of history, art and Inquisition ghosts. Open 10–1 and 3:30–6:30, 20 trains a day from Atocha or Chamartin stations. Upon arrival, get right on the bus that takes visitors from the station to the palace.
Avila—With perfectly preserved medieval walls (to climb them, enter through the gardens of the Parador) and several fine churches and monasteries, this is a popular side trip from Madrid. Just beyond El Escorial you could do them together in one day, spending the night in Avila and carrying on to Segovia (4 buses daily) or Salamanca (4 trains daily). Tourist info (9:30–1:30, 4:00–7:00) is opposite the cathedral on the main plaza.

Itinerary Options
If jet lag isn't a problem and there's no flea market or bullfight to hang around for, you may be able to see all you want of Madrid in Days 2 and 3. This means you could skip Day 4 using it as a free day to plug in later in your trip. Nearly any three week tour can use a slack day sooner or later. If it turns out you don't need it, enjoy that extra Madrid day at the end of your trip.

Trains from Madrid—From Madrid's Chamartin Station to Barcelona (4 a day, 10–13 hours); Paris (8 daily, 12–14 hours). From Atocha station to: Lisbon (5; 10–13 hours), Algeciras (2; 12 hours), Cordoba (5; 5–7 hours), Granada (2; 8–10 hours), Segovia (12; 1½–2 hours). From Norte station (Príncipe Pío) to Salamanca (5; 2½ hours).

DAY 5
MADRID—SEGOVIA—SALAMANCA

Today we leave the big city for historic Segovia. Late in the afternoon
we'll carry on to Salamanca to enjoy a romantic evening on Spain's love-
liest town square.

Suggested Schedule

8:00	Leave Madrid.
10:30	Arrive Segovia. Tour Cathedral, Alcazar, Aqueduct.
1:00	Lunch—roast suckling pig under the Aqueduct.
3:00	Drive to Salamanca, set up.
6:00	Tour Cathedrals.
8:00	Dinner and evening on Plaza Mayor.

Transportation Madrid—Segovia (50 miles) By car, leave Madrid on
Calle Princesa in the direction of La Coruna on N-VI. Turn right at Vil-
lalaba onto N-601. The trip takes about 90 minutes.

By bus, leave station La Sepuldevana (Calle Pasco de Florida 11, metro:
Norte). There are 4 buses a day (8:00, 11:45, 15:00, and 19:30) with connections to Avila.

There are 12 trains a day leaving from Atocha station.

Segovia
Just 50 miles from Madrid, Segovia boasts a great Roman aqueduct, a cathedral, and a castle. It's well worth the better part of a day. (Elevation
3,000 feet, pop. 55,000, tourist info: Plaza Mayor #8.)

Sightseeing Highlights
▲▲**Roman Aqueduct**—Built by the Romans who ruled Spain for over
500 years, this 2,000 year old "Acueducto Romano" is 2,500 feet long,
100 feet high, has 118 arches, yet was made without any mortar. Climb
the stairs at one end to the top of the old city wall where you'll get a
good look at the channel that carried the stream of water into the city
until the beginning of our century.
▲**The Cathedral**—Segovia's cathedral was Spain's last major Gothic
building. Embellished to the hilt with pinnacles and flying buttresses,
this is a great example of the final "over-ripe" stage of Gothic called
"Flamboyant." (open 10–7).
▲**The Alcazar**—This is a Disney-esque exaggeration of the old castle
which burned down 100 years ago. Still fun to explore and worthwhile
for the view. (open 10–7).

Accommodations
Budget "Fondas" abound around the Plaza Franco. We enjoyed
Acueducto (Avenida Padre Claret 10).

Food
Roast suckling pig (cochinillo asado) is Segovia's culinary claim to fame,
and well worth a splurge here (or in Toledo or Salamanca). The Meson
de Candido (Plaza del Azoguejo 5, near the aqueduct) is one of the top
restaurants in Castile. Also very good is Casa Amado (Ladieda 9). The
best bars cluster around Plaza Franco. Try those on Calle de Infantes
Isabella. Jose Maria (Cronista Lecea 11) and Tasca la Posada (Judería Vieja
1) are also good.

Transportation: Segovia—Salamanca (100 miles)
In the afternoon we'll start the easy 2–3 hour drive to Salamanca with a
chance to see Avila en route. When you arrive in Salamanca, park your
car behind the Puente Nueva (bridge) and leave it. Parking is difficult
and the town is small enough to manage on foot. General warning:
Leave nothing of value in your car—especially in large tourist-area car
parks. The theft problem almost vanishes in small untouristed places.

Public transportation from Segovia to Salamanca is messy, so if you're
traveling without a car we'd recommend seeing Segovia as a half day
side trip from Madrid and going directly from Madrid to Salamanca.
There are 6 buses a day from Madrid (4½ hours). The 3½ hour train
leaves 4 times a day from Madrid's station Príncipe Pío, via Avila (8:40,
9:25, 15:40, 19:10). Arriving in Salamanca, the train station is a 15-
minute walk from the center. A bus will take you to the Plaza Mayor.
Train info tel. 212–454.

Salamanca
Salamanca is Spain's city of grace. Covered with warm harmonious
sandstone architecture, maintaining its university atmosphere, enjoying
its unrivaled main square and thankfully without the noisy modern
sprawl that plagues so many other cities, this is a great place to spend
the night and half a day.

Sightseeing Highlights
▲▲▲**Plaza Mayor**—"The" Spanish Plaza, this central square, built in
1755, is really the best in Spain. A fine place to nurse a cup of coffee and
watch the world go by.
▲▲**The Cathedral**—Actually two cathedrals—both richly
ornamented—side by side. The "new" cathedral was begun in 1513
with Renaissance and Baroque parts added later. The old cathedral goes
back to the 12th century. (Open 10–1:45, 4–7:45).
▲▲**The University**—Founded in 1230, the Salamanca University is the
oldest in Spain and was one of Europe's finest centers of learning for
400 years. Columbus came here for help with his nautical calculations
and today many Americans enjoy its excellent summer program. Open
Mon-Sat, 9:30–1:30, 4–6. Explore the old lecture halls were many of
Spain's Golden Age heroes studied.
Salamanca's Blood Red Graffiti—As you walk through the old town
you may see red writing on the walls. For centuries students have
celebrated their PhD graduation by killing and roasting a bull, having a
big feast, and writing their names and new title on a town wall with the

bull's blood. While this is now "forbidden," some traditions refuse to die.

Accommodations
Try to stay near or on the Plaza Mayor. We like the Hotel Gran Vía (La Rosa 4, inexpensive and very central). The Gran Hotel on Plaza Poeta Inglesias 6 (near Plaza Mayor, tel. 21–3500) offers luxurious doubles for $25.

Food
There are plenty of good and inexpensive places between the Plaza Mayor and the Gran Vía. Try Las Torres (Plaza Mayor 26), Novelty (Plaza Mayor, great coffee), Mesón de Cervantes (Plaza Mayor, good tapas, sit outside or upstairs, young crowd), La Covachuela (Plaza Mercado 24), and several places on Calle Bermejeros (La Taberna de Pilatos, de la Reina, and more). For a special dinner go to Chez Victor (Espoz y Mina 22, closed Sunday and Monday).

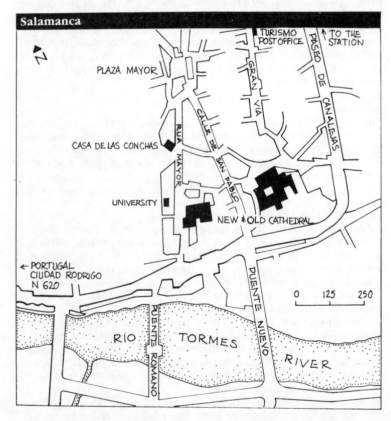

DAY 6
SALAMANCA—CIUDAD RODRIGO—COIMBRA

After a morning look at Salamanca's university, we'll travel to the old cultural center of Portugal, Coimbra. En route we'll stop to see a wonderfully preserved and overlooked frontier hill town.

Suggested Schedule	
8:00	Breakfast on Plaza Mayor, Salamanca.
9:30	Explore Salamanca University.
10:30	Drive to Ciudad Rodrigo.
12:00	Wander around old town and the wall. Lunch.
2:00	Travel to Coimbra.
6:00	Explore old town, Coimbra.
8:00	Dinner.

Transportation: Salamanca—Ciudad Rodrigo (60 miles)
An easy, boring, but fast drive. There are six buses a day, but from Ciudad Rodrigo the connection to the border is terrible—only one a day. By train, five trains a day go from Salamanca-Ciudad Rodrigo-Fuentes de Onoro-Guarda. Good connections from Guarda to Coimbra and Lisbon.

Ciudad Rodrigo
This beautiful old town of 16,000 people caps a hill overlooking the Río Agueda. Spend an hour wandering among the Renaissance mansions that line its streets and exploring the 18th century town walls. From these walls you can look into Portugal. The castle is now a luxurious parador (a parador is a government-operated hotel, often a historic castle; all have restaurants). A reasonable way to enjoy this elegance is to splurge for a lunch here. Otherwise head for the Plaza Mayor for a bite to eat. Try coffee and tapas at El Sanatorio (#13, Plaza Mayor).

Ciudad Rodrigo's cathedral has a special surprise. You'll see a man outside a small door who, for a small price, will take you on a walk through a series of 12th-Century groin vaults ornamented with stone carvings racy enough to make Hugh Hefner blush. Who said 'when you've seen one Gothic church you've seen 'em all?'

Transportation: Ciudad Rodrigo—Coimbra (150 miles)
By car the drive is fast, easy, uncrowded and, until Guarda, fairly dull. After Guarda the road takes you through the beautiful Serra da Estrela Mountains. Remember, set your watch back one hour as you cross into Portugal. Park the car and leave it (this is an "on foot" town) along the river on Avda Emidio Navarro. Leave absolutely *nothing* inside.

There are five trains daily from Ciudad Rodrigo to Coimbra (two are coming direct from Paris, and three require a change in Guarda). The bus station is a mile from the center down Avda Fernao Magalhaes. Six or seven buses leave Rodrigo daily to Spain or Lisbon.

Coimbra—Orientation

Coimbra (pronounced KWEEM-bra) is a small town of winding streets
set on the side of a hill. The high point is the old university. From there
little lanes dribble down to the main business and shopping street, Rua
de Ferreira Borges and the Mondego River. If school is in, Coimbra
bustles. During school holidays, it's more sleepy.

There are two train stations: A & B. Major trains all stop at B (big).
From there it's easy to catch a small train to the very central A station
(just "take the A train"). The tourist info office (Largo da Portagem, tel.
25576, open M-Sat 9–8, Sun 10:30–12:30, 2–6) and plenty of good
budget rooms are near the A station (train info tel. 34998).

From the Largo da Portagem (main square) everything is within an
easy walk. The old town spreads out like an amphitheater—timeworn
houses, shops, and stairways, all leading up to the old university.

Accommodations

The more comfortable rooms lie on Avenida Emidio Navarro along the
river. Try Hotel Astoria (at #21, tel. 22055, $20 dbls, front rooms are too
noisy). Cheaper and more interesting places are in the old quarter especially on Rua da Sota (leaving Largo da Portagem to the west). There are
plenty of $10 doubles. Try Pensão Rivoli (Praça do Comercio 27, tel.
25550) or Residencia Parque (Avda Navarro 42, tel. 29202, river view,
English spoken).

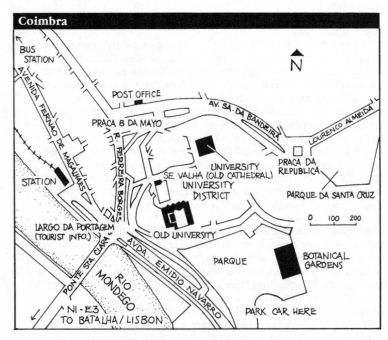

DAY 7
COIMBRA—BATALHA—NAZARE/
SÃO MARTINHO DO PORTO

Today we'll tour the historic Coimbra University, then travel to the huge Gothic monastery at Batalha, finally arriving at our beach town headquarters on the Atlantic.

Suggested Schedule

8:00	Breakfast in hotel or with busy locals in a bar on Rua Ferreira Berges.
8:30	Enjoy a shady morning in the old town alleys and shops. It's about a 15- minute walk to the university. Stop by the old cathedral on your way.
10:00	Tour the university.
12:00	Lunch outside Coimbra. Leave Coimbra, crossing the bridge over the Mondego River. Turn right onto Ave. Joao das Negras. Stop at #10 Restaurant Alfredo for a great budget lunch—three courses for under $5.
1:30	Drive to Batalha. You'll pass the Roman ruins of Conimbriga and castles at Pombal and Leiria. None of great importance but each interesting if you're interested.
3:30	Batalha Abbey (Monastery of Sta. Maria).
5:30	Drive to São Martinho do Porto.

Coimbra
Don't be fooled by the ugly suburbs and monotonous concrete apartment buildings that surround the town. Coimbra was Portugal's most important city for 200 years and second only to Lisbon culturally and historically. It led Portugal while the Moors still controlled Lisbon. Only as Portugal's maritime fortunes rose was Coimbra surpassed by the port towns of Lisbon and Porto. Today Coimbra is still Portugal's third largest city (70,000). It has its oldest and most prestigious university (founded 1307) and a great old quarter—with the flavor of a colorful Moroccan Kasbah. The view from the south end of Santa Clara bridge is a great introduction to this town.

Sightseeing Highlights
Old Cathedral (Se Velha)—This is probably the most impressive Romanesque building in Portugal. Built like a bulky fortress with an interesting Flamboyant Gothic altarpiece inside.
▲Old University—Coimbra's university was modeled after the Bologna University (Europe's first, 1139). It's a stately, three-winged building located beautifully overlooking the city. At first Law, Medicine, Grammar and Logic were taught. Then, with Portugal's seafaring orientation, Astronomy and Geometry were added. The library is a rich collection of thousands of old books and historic documents surrounded by gilded ceilings and baroque halls. The inlaid rosewood reading tables and the shelves of precious woods are a reminder that Portugal's wealth

was great and it came from far away. Enjoy the panoramic view from
here and imagine being a student in Coimbra 500 years ago.

Don't miss the Manueline-style chapel and its lavish organ loft. (Open
10-2 and 5-7, ring the doorbell to get in).

Transportation: Coimbra—Batalha—São Martinho/Nazare (60 miles)

By car, you'll travel to Batalha on highway N1, continuing to São Martinho on E50. Traffic on both roads is often terrible. The train goes
seven times daily from Coimbra to Nazare with a change in Figueira da
Foz. Batalha is reached better by bus. You'll go to Leiria first (1¾ hours)
and catch one of eight daily buses from there to Alcobaca, via Batalha.
From Batalha to São Martinho or Nazare requires a change in Alcobaca.

São Martinho and Nazare, just 8 miles apart, are connected by regular
buses.

Batalha—the Monastery of Santa María

This is Portugal's greatest architectural achievement and a symbol of its
national pride. Batalha was built in 1385 to celebrate a Portugese victory
which freed her from Spanish rule. Batalha means "battle."

The greatness of Portugal's age of discovery shines brightly in the
giant but harmonious mix of Gothic and Manueline styles—the Royal
Cloisters, which manage to combine the sensibility of Gothic with the
elaborate decoration of the fancier Manueline style, and the Chapter
House with its frighteningly broad vaults. This heavy ceiling was considered so dangerous to build (it collapsed twice) that only prisoners
condemned to death were allowed to work on it. Today it's considered
stable enough to be the home of the Portugese tomb of the unknown
soldier. Also visit the Founder's Chapel with many royal tombs,
including Henry the Navigator's.

Open 9-7 daily. The Batalha Abbey is great—but nothing else at this
stop is. See it, then head on out to the coast.

Nazare and São Martinho do Porto—Accommodations

Nazare is a fine homebase town off season, but it's just too crowded in
the summer. If you do spend the night, we slept and ate well at the
Pensão-Restaurate Ribamar (Rua Gomes Freire 9, at the west end of the
promenade). Finding a room is almost too easy. You'll be met by plenty
of people renting private rooms. Always inspect any room before ac-
cepting it.

To avoid the crowds and enjoy a quiet piece of beach, a small village
eight miles south is a better stop—São Martinho do Porto. There's
tourist info right on the beach promenade in the São Martinho town
center. Our favorite accommodation is the Hotel Parque (Av. Marchal
Carmona, tel. 98505, $25 doubles with stucco ceilings and a peaceful
park). There are several cheaper pensions nearby.

To really escape, go to tiny Salir do Porto nearby. This village has a
few private rooms (quarto) to rent and virtually no tourism.

DAY 8
SÃO MARTINHO/NAZARE—BEACH TIME AND CIRCULAR EXCURSION

After all the traveling you've done, it's time for an easy day and some fun in the sun. Between two nights in our beach town, we'll take a small trip inland, spend the afternoon soaking up the sun, and savor an evening with enough salty fishing village atmosphere to make you pucker.

Suggested Schedule	
8:00	Breakfast at hotel.
8.30	Drive through countryside, visiting the roadside windmill, the wine museum and Alcobaca (town and monastery).
1:00	Lunch in Nazare, ride funicular up to Sitio, free time on beaches.
7:00	Seafood dinner—shrimp and vinho verde—watch the boats come in and the sun set in Nazare. Then return to São Martinho, your quiet homebase.

Circular Excursion through the Countryside
Leaving São Martinho (or Nazare) you'll drive through eucalyptus groves (suddenly the world smells like a coughdrop!) toward Alcobaca past windmill after windmill. Portugal has more working windmills than even Holland. One of them just off the Nazare-Alcobaca road is obviously eager for guests. Tour it. It's like a cross between a giant white salt shaker and a helicopter trying its best to take off. With its weird ceramic whistle pots lashed to the sails, it whirrs an eerie Wizard of Oz hurricane sound. Upstairs, the miller will demonstrate how the entire top can be winched around to face the shifting wind, and how effectively this clean air power is harnessed to grind his corn.

The nearby town of Alcobaca is famous for its church, the biggest in Portugal—historic but mediocre and barely worth a visit except to notice how much better Batalha, built 200 years later, is. But Alcobaca's market will always shine brightly in my memory. It houses the Old World happily under its huge steel and glass dome. Inside, black-clad, dried-apple-faced women choose fish, chicks, birds, and rabbits from death row. Figs, melons, bushels of grain and nuts—a caveman's Safeway. Buying a picnic is a perfect excuse to take a ride on this magic market carpet.

Just outside of town you'll find the local co-operative winery. Its tour, much more "hands on" than French winery tours, is a walk through mountains of centrifuged, strained and drained grapes—all well on the road to fermentation. The tour climaxes with a climb to the top of one of twenty half-buried 80,000-gallon tanks—all busy fermenting. Look out! I stuck my head into the manhole-sized top vent and just as I focused on the rich bubbling grape stew, I was walloped silly by a wine vapor-punch.

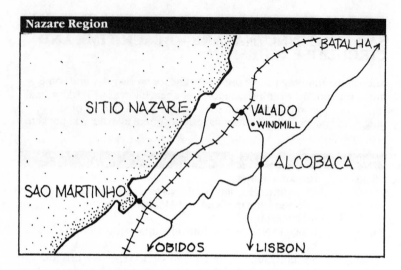

Nazare Region

Back in Nazare you'll be greeted by the energetic applause of the forever surf and big plates of smiling steamed shrimp.

Nazare

In the summer it seems that each of this famous town's 10,000 inhabitants is in the tourist trade. Nazare is a hit with tour groups and masses of Lisbon day-trippers who come up to see traditionally-clad fishermen do everything as traditionally as possible. The beach promenade is a congested tangle of oily sunbathers, hustlers, plastic souvenirs, over-priced restaurants and romantic fishing boats.

Off season, however, Nazare is almost empty of tourists, inexpensive, colorful and relaxed.

Anytime of year it's worth a look. Prowl the beach, ride the funicular to the white-washed cliff-top old village of Sitio for the staggering coastal view. Check out the traditional outfits the locals still wear. Be on the beach when the fishing boats come in at about 8:00pm.

DAY 9
SÃO MARTINHO/NAZARE—OBIDOS—LISBON

Today we travel about 60 miles, leaving the beach village to spend a few hours in Portugal's cutest walled city, enjoying what is probably Portugal's best seafood for lunch, and then driving into Lisbon.

Suggested Schedule

8:00	Breakfast, drive to Obidos.
9:00	Explore Obidos.
11:30	Drive to nearby Ericeira. Lunch.
1:00	Drive to Lisbon, set up.
4:00	Explore Alfama, dinner there.

Transportation: Nazare/São Martinho—Obidos—Lisbon (60 miles)

Transportation becomes more regular as we approach Lisbon. Trains and buses go almost hourly from Nazare—São Martinho—Obidos—Lisbon. While Ericeira is served by buses via Torres Vedras and Mafra and regularly from Lisbon, it's probably worthwhile only if you have a car.

Both Nazare and São Martinho are on the main Lisbon-Porto train line. The Nazare station is three miles out of town near Valado (easy bus connection) and São Martinho's is about one mile from town. There are several buses a day from both towns to Batalha/Coimbra and to Lisbon via Obidos/Torres Vedras.

Obidos

This medieval walled town was Portugal's "wedding city"—the perfect gift for kings to give their queens. Today it is preserved in its entirety as a national monument, surviving off tourism.

The postcard town sits atop a hill, its perfect 40-foot high wall corralling a bouquet of narrow lanes and flower decked white-washed houses. Walk around the wall, peek into the castle (now a lavish pousada—tel. 95105, $30 doubles), lose yourself for awhile in this lived-in open air museum of medieval city-planning. It's fun to wander the back lanes, study the solid centuries-old houses. . . and think about progress. There's a small museum, an interesting Renaissance church with lovely azulejo walls inside and, outside the walls, an aqueduct and a windmill.

Obidos is crowded in July and August. Filter out the tourists and it's still great.

Obidos is tough on the budget. The pousada is a wonderful splurge for lunch. Otherwise pick up a picnic at the grocery store near the main gate. If you have time to spend the night you'll enjoy the town without tourists. The pousada is a good value, as is the Estalagem do Convente, Rua Dr. Joao de Orvelas (tel. 95217, doubles $20, just outside the old quarter). For cheap intimacy ask around for "quartos" (Bed and Breakfast). The Obidos tourist info is open from 9am-8pm. Pick up their handy town map listing B&B places.

A Side Trip to Seafood Paradise

Seafood lovers rave about an otherwise uninteresting town called
Ericeira. Just a few miles west from Torres Vedras, this place is a great
lunch stop. Dozens of bars and restaurants pull the finest lobster, giant
crab, mussels and fish out of the sea and serve them up fresh and cheap.
$5 will buy you a meal fit for Neptune. Most places are on the main
street.

There are good beaches just a few miles north and south of Ericeira.
Buses go several times daily between Lisbon, Sintra, and Ericeira.

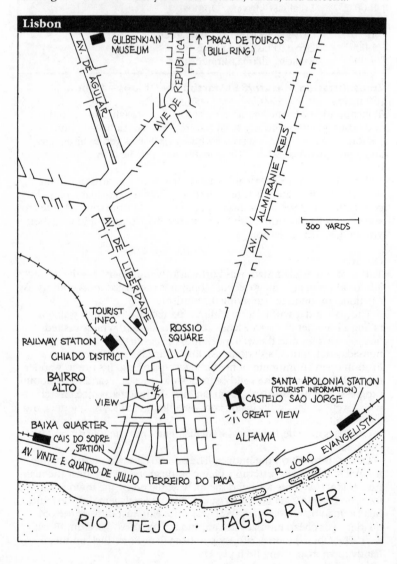

Lisbon—Orientation

Lisbon is easy. Its prime attractions are mostly within walking distance
of the Rossio Square. The Rossio is the heart of Lisbon with plenty of
buses, subways and cheap taxis leaving in all directions.

Between the Rossio and the harbor is the lower city, Baixa, with its
checkerboard street plan, elegant architecture, bustling shops and many
cafes.

On a hill to the west of the Rossio is the old and noble shopping district of Chiado. Look for shoes, bags, and leather goods on Rua Garett
and Rua Carmo, and gold and silver on the Rua do Ouro (gold street).
Stores are furnished like museums—don't miss the palatial Grandes Ar-
mazenas do Chiado (Rua do Carmo #2), the Portuguese answer to
London's Harrods. Above that is the Bairro Alto (upper quarter) with its
dark bars, hidden restaurants, and many *fado* places.

East of Baixa is another hill blanketed by the medieval Alfama quarter
and capped by the Castelo São Jorge. The castelo offers the best view of
Lisbon and a great way to get oriented.

Avenida Liberdade is the "Champs Elysées" of Lisbon, connecting the
old lower town with the newer upper end.

The main Tourist Information office is at the lower end of Ave. Liberdade in the Palacio Foz at Praça Restauradores. (Mon-Sat 9:00–8:00, Sun
10–6, tel. 363643; 24-hour telephone service—893–689). It's friendly
and helpful. I even got help pronouncing my basic Portugese phrases.
There are also offices at Castelo São Jorge, in the Apolonia station and at
the airport.

Banks, the Post Office, airlines, and travel agents are all along the Ave.
Liberdade. American Express is in the "Star Travel" travel agency (tel.
539871, open M-F 9–12:30 and 2–6, helpful) at Avda Sidonio País #4A
and at #14 Praça dos Restauradores.

Lisbon has four train stations (see map). Santa Apolonia is the major
station, handling all international trains and trains going to north and
east Portugal. It's just past the Alfama, with good bus connections to the
town center, tourist info, a room finding service and 24-hour money
change service. Barreiro station, a 5-minute ferry ride across the Tagus
River from Praça do Comercio, is for trains to the Algarve and points
south. Rossio station goes to Sintra and the west, and Cais do Sodre station handles the 30-minute rides to Cascaís and Estoril.

The airport, just 5 miles northeast of downtown, has good bus connections to town, cheap taxis, a 24-hour bank and tourist info, and a
guarded parking lot ($1.50/day). Tel. 802060.

Lisbon has fine public transportation. Don't drive your car in the
city—park it safely and leave it. Leave nothing valuable in your car and
park it in a guarded lot (ask your hotel for advice).

The Lisbon subway is simple, clean, fast, and cheap. It runs from
6:00–1:00am. The big letter "M" marks metro stops.

The bus system is great. Pick up the "Guía dos Transportes Públicos
de Lisboa e Região" for specifics on buses in and around Lisbon.

Lisbon's vintage trolley system is as fun and colorful as San Francisco's.
Line #28 from Graca to Prazeres offers a great Lisbon joy ride.

Accommodations
Finding a room in Lisbon is easy. Cheap and charming ride the same
teeter-totter, so the neighborhood you choose will generally determine
the mix you get. If you arrive late, or in July or August, the room-
finding services in the station and at the airport are very helpful. Otherwise, just wander through the district of your choice and find your own
bed.

Many pensions ($10–20 doubles) are around the Rossio and in the
side streets near the Ave. Liberdade. Quieter and more colorful places
are in the Baírro Alto and around the Castle São Jorge, but those areas
are a little on the sleazy side at night.

For splurges, we've enjoyed the old world Hotel Borges (Rua Garret
108, tel. 361–951, in the Chiado area, $25 doubles); Palace Hotel (grand
old atmosphere with crystal chandeliers and heavy furniture, on Rua 1
de Dezembro, tel. 360151, doubles $35–40, in center between Rossio
and Restauradores); Residencia Caravella (Rua Ferreira Lapa 38, next to
Ave. Duque de Loule, 1100 Lisbon, tel. 539011, comfortable hotel, central, English spoken); and the popular York House (also called
Residencia Inglesa, pleasant English atmosphere in old villa with garden
out toward Belem district at Rua Janeles Verdes #32, tel. 662–435, $30
doubles).

When searching for a pension, here are some things to remember:
singles are nearly as expensive as doubles; many buildings have several
different pensions, addresses like 26–3° mean street #26, third floor
(which is fourth floor in American terms).

To enjoy a more peaceful, old beach resort atmosphere away from the
big city intensity, establish headquarters at Cascais, just 14 miles away.
Cheap 30-minute trains go downtown several times an hour.

Food
Lisbon has several great restaurant districts: Baírro Alto has plenty of
small, fun and cheap places. Go to the Jardin de São Pedro terrace for a
light and quick food stall meal. The Alfama has many good places along
the main drag, Rua São Pedro on Largo de São Miguel, and a great no-
name hole-in-the-wall working-class lunch place just across the street
from the Miradouro de Santa Luzia. Near the Ave. Liberdade on Rua das
Portas de Santo Antão and Rua dos Correiros you'll find countless little
restaurants. And, finally, don't miss a chance to go purely local with
hundreds of Portugese families having salad, fries, chicken and wine at
the "Feira Popular." More on eating is built into the sample schedules.

DAY 10
LISBON

This is a day for strolling and browsing through Lisbon's tangled jungle of streets and shops.

Suggested Schedule	
8:00	Breakfast in your hotel.
9:00	Shopping and browsing in the old Baixa and Chiado quarters.
1:00	Lunch along Lisbon's "eating lane" (Rua das Portas de Santo Antão), or at the top of the Alfama with a view from Castelo São Jorge.
3:00	Stroll through the Alfama.
8:00	Dinner, with harbor view.
10:00	An evening of drink and drone in a Baírro Alto *fado* restaurant ($10–15).

Lisbon

Lisbon is a wonderful mix of now and then. Old wooden trollies shiver up and down its hills, bird-stained statues mark grand squares, and people sip coffee in art nouveau cafes.

Present-day Lisbon is explained by its past. While her history goes back to Roman and Moorish days, her glory days were the 15th and 16th centuries when explorers like Vasco da Gama opened up new trade routes making Lisbon Europe's richest city. This economic boom brought the flamboyant art boom called the Manueline period. Later in the early 18th century, the riches of Brazil boosted Lisbon even higher. Then, in 1755, a tremendous earthquake leveled the city killing over 20% of its people.

Lisbon was rebuilt under the energetic leadership of the Marquis Pombal. The grandeur of pre-earthquake Lisbon survives only in Belem, the Alfama and in the Baírro Alto districts. The Pombal-designed downtown is on a strict grid plan, symmetrical, with broad boulevards and square squares.

While the earthquake flattened a lot of buildings, and its colonial empire is long gone, Lisbon's heritage is alive and well. Barely elegant outdoor cafes, exciting art, entertaining museums, the saltiest sailors' quarter in Europe, and much more, all at bargain basement prices, make Lisbon an Iberian highlight.

Thieves abound in Lisbon. Be on a theft alert everywhere, but particularly in the Alfama, Baírro Alto and at night.

Sightseeing Highlights—Day 10

▲▲▲**Alfama**—This most colorful sailors' quarter in Europe was the Visigothic birthplace of Lisbon, a rich district during the Arabic period and then the salty home of Lisbon's fisherfolk. One of the few areas to survive the 1755 earthquake, the Alfama is a cobbled cornucopia of Old World color. Visit during the busy midmorning market time, or in the late afternoon/early evening when the streets teem with locals.

Wander deep. This urban jungle's roads are squeezed to tangled and confused alleys; bent houses comfort each other in their romantic shabbiness and the air drips with laundry and the smell of clams and raw fish. You'll probably get lost but that doesn't matter—unless you're trying to stay found. Poke aimlessly, sample ample grapes, avoid rabid-looking dogs, peek through windows. This is our favorite European cranny.

"Electrico" street cars #10, 11, and 26 go to the Alfama. On Tuesdays and Saturday mornings the "Feira da Ladra" flea market rages on the Campo de Santa Clara (bus #12, trolley #28).

▲**Castelo São Jorge**—The city castle with a history going back to Roman days caps the hill above the Alfama and offers the finest view possible of Lisbon. Use this perch to orient yourself.

▲**Fado**—The fado, mournfully beautiful, haunting ballads about lost sailors, broken hearts, and sad romance, is one of Lisbon's favorite late-night pastimes. Be careful, this is also one of those cultural cliches that all too often become tourist traps. The Alfama has many fado bars but most are terribly touristy. The Baírro Alto is your best bet. Things don't start 'til 10:00 and then take an hour or two to warm up. A fado performance isn't cheap (plan to spend around $10) and many fado joints require dinner. Ask at your hotel for advice.

Food

The smaller pensions actually serve breakfast in bed since they have no dining area. Or try one of the traditional coffeehouses (like the Cafe Suiza) on the Rossio.

The best pastry and delicious hot chocolate are at Ferrari (Rua Nova do Almada 93). The world's greatest selection of port wines is neaby at Solar do Vinho do Porto, on Rua São Pedro de Alcantara 45. For a small price, you can taste any of 250 different ports.

The "eating lane"—Rua das Portas de Santo Antao—a hundred yards east of Praça Restauradores, is a galloping gourmet's heaven with all kinds of eateries to choose from. The seafood is great. Rather than siesta, have a small black coffee (called a "bica") in a shady cafe on the Ave. Liberdade.

Another lunch option is to take a taxi to the Miradouro de Santa Luzia square at the top of the Alfama in the bustling no-name fisherman's hangout just across the street from the square. Shellfish and beer are nearly required here. Castelo São Jorge is just up the hill.

Drop into a few Alfama bars, have an aperitif, taste the "blanco seco"—the local dry wine. Make a friend, pet a chicken, read the graffiti, study the humanity ground between the cobbles.

For dinner with a great harbor view, try Faz Figueira (Rua do Paraíso 15B) or its neighbors in the Alfama. For a simple atmospheric meal (about $4) check out the fishermen's bars on Rua Nova Trinidade in the Baírro Alto.

DAY 11
THE ART AND HISTORY OF LISBON

After yesterday's plunge into the Lisbon jungle, today we'll concentrate on the "sights" of Lisbon, the museum and the architecture recalling the glory days of Portugese history.

Suggested Schedule

8:00	Breakfast in hotel or in one of the bars on Ave. Liberdade.
9:30	Catch bus to Gulbenkian Museum.
12:00	There's a good cafeteria in the museum but we prefer one of Lisbon's best traditional restaurants, the O Policia, just behind the museum on Rua de Sa da Bandeira 162 (closed Sundays). Very popular with locals, unknown to tourists, great seafood, meals around $8.
2:00	Taxi, bus or streetcar to Belem to see the glories of Lisbon's golden age. See the Monastery of the Jeronimos, Monument to the Discoveries, and Belem Tower for sure. The coach, maritime and pop art museums if you like.
8:00	Dinner—how about supper in the azulejo-covered cellar of the Bar Trinidade in the Bairro Alto (Rua Trinidade 10).

Sightseeing Highlights

▲▲**Gulbenkian Museum**—The best of Lisbon's 40 museums. The Armenian oil tycoon, Gulbenkian, gave his art collection (or "harem" as he called it) to Portugal in gratitude for the hospitable asylum granted him here during WWII. Now this great collection spanning 2,000 years of art is displayed in a classy and comfortable modern building.

Pick up a guidebook in the foyer. Great Egyptian and Greek sections, masterpieces by Rembrandt, Rubens, Renoir, Rodin, and more. Good cafeteria, cheap and air-conditioned, nice gardens. Take bus lines 15, 30, 31, 41, 46, or 56 from downtown. Open Tues-Sun 10-5, Wed and Sat until 7:00 in summer.

▲▲▲**Belem District**—The Belem District, 4 miles from downtown is a pincushion of important sights from Portugal's Golden Age, when Vasco da Gama and company made her Europe's richest power. (Bus #12, 29, 43; streetcar #15, 16, 17 from Praça Comercio; or taxi).

The Belem Tower, the only purely Manueline building in Portugal (built 1515), protected Lisbon's harbor and today symbolizes the voyages that made her powerful. This was the last sight sailors saw as they left and the first one they'd see when they returned loaded down with gold, diamonds and spices. (Open Tues-Sun 9:00-7:00).

The giant Monument to the Discoveries was built in 1960 to honor Henry the Navigator who died 500 years earlier. Huge statues of Henry and Portugal's leading explorers line the giant concrete prow.

The Monastery of Jeronimos is possibly Portugal's most exciting building. In the giant church and its cloisters, notice how nicely the Manueline style combines Gothic and Renaissance features with motifs

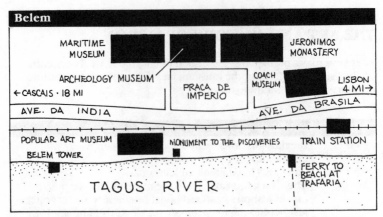

from the sea—the source of the wealth which made this art possible.
Don't miss the elegant cloisters—by far my favorite in Europe (open
Tues-Sun 10-7).

The Belem museums are somewhere between dull and mediocre de-
pending on your interests. The coach museum has over 70 carriages
from the 18th century. The pop art museum takes you one province at a
time through Portugal's folk art. The maritime museum is a cut above
the average European maritime museum. Don't miss it if you're a sailor.
Museum Nacional de Arte Antigua—Paintings and rich furniture
from the days when Portugal owned the world. (Rua das Janeles Verdes
9, open 10-1, 2:30-5. Closed Mondays.)
▲**Bullfights**—The Portugese "tourada" could be considered a humane
version of the Spanish "corrida"—the Portugese don't kill the bull.
After an equestrian prelude, a colorfully-clad eight-man team enters the
ring. The leader prompts the bull to charge and he meets the bull right
between the padded horns. As he hangs onto the bull's head, his bud-
dies try to wrestle it to the ground. The season lasts from Easter through
October and you're most likely to see a fight in Lisbon, Estoril or on the
Algarve. Fights start late in the evening. Get schedules at the tourist info.
▲▲**The Popular Fair**—By all means spend an evening at Lisbon's
"Feira Popular," which rages nightly 'til 1:00am, May through September. Located on Ave. da Republica at the Entrecampos metro stop,
this fair bustles with Portugese families at play. Pay the 25-cent entry
fee, then enjoy rides, munchies, great people-watching, entertainment,
music, basic Portugese fun. Have dinner here, among chattering families
with endless food and wine paraded frantically in every direction. Fried
ducks drip, barbecues spit and dogs squirt the legs of chairs while,
somehow, local lovers ignore everything but each other's eyes.

DAY 12
SIDE TRIPS FROM LISBON

The area to the west of Lisbon is well worth a busy day. A circular tour,
Lisbon-Sintra-Capo da Roca-Cascaís-Estoril-Lisbon, is a great look at
some small but elegant towns that history has passed by.

Suggested Schedule

8:00	Breakfast and travel from Lisbon to Sintra.
9:00–2:00	Sintra, town, national palace, Moorish ruins, Pena Palace, Monserrate Park, picnic.
2:00	Drive to Capo da Roca.
4:00	Free time in Estoril and Cascais.
8:00	Dinner in Cascais or back in Lisbon.

**Transportation: Circular Excursion, Lisbon—Sintra—Capo da
Roca—Cascais—Lisbon**
This is very easy and most fun by car, and might be a day when even
bus and train travelers would enjoy a rental car (several companies on
Ave. Liberdade).

Public transportation is also good. Trains go from Lisbon to Sintra (50
min.) and Cascais (30 min.) three times an hour, and buses connect
points further west. Buses go regularly between Sintra, Capo da Roca
and Cascais.

For the best swimming around, catch the bus from Lisbon (3 a day)
30 miles south to the Arrabida Coast.

Sintra
Just 12 miles north of Lisbon, this was the summer escape of Portugal's
kings. Byron called it a "glorious Eden." It's a lush playground of castles,
palaces, sweeping coastal views and exotic gardens. You could easily
spend a whole day here.

In the town (10 minutes from the train station) tour the strange but
lavish Palacio Nacional. Then drive, climb or taxi to the thousand-year-
old Moorish castle ruins. Lost in an enchanted forest and alive with
winds of the past, these ruins are a castle-lover's dream come true.
Great place for a picnic with a panoramic Atlantic view.

Nearby is the magical hill-capping Pena Palace. Portugal's German-
born Prince Ferdinand hired a German architect to build him a fantasy
castle mixing elements of German and Portugese style. He got a crazy
fortified salad of Mad Ludwig, Gothic, Arabic, Moorish, Renaissance,
and Manueline architectural bits and decorative pieces. The Palace, built
in the 1840s, is preserved just as it was when the Royal family fled Portugal in 1910. (Open 10–5, closed Tuesdays).

Also in the area is the wonderful garden of Monserrate. If you like
tropical plants and exotic landscaping, this is definitely for you.

Nearly everyone who visits Sintra is day tripping from Lisbon. It is a
fine place to spend a night. The Pensão Nova Sintra and the Estalagem
da Raposa are two of several good—and nostalgic—hotels in São Pedro.

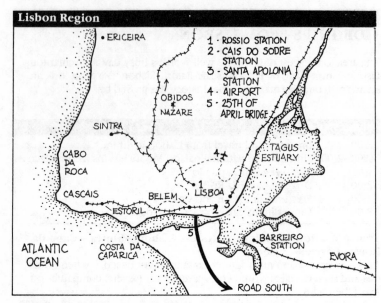

Colares, also near Sintra, is another sleepy place with a salty breeze. We enjoyed the Pensão Vareza, right downtown (tel. 299–0008).

Capo da Roca
The wind-beaten Capo da Roca is the westernmost point in Europe. This Continental Land's End has a fun little shop and info booth where you can have a drink and pick up your "proof of being here" diploma. Nearby, the Praia (beach) das Macas is a good place for wind, waves, sand and sun. Buses go regularly between Capo da Roca, Sintra, and Cascais.

Cascais and Estoril
Before the rise of the Algarve, these towns were the haunt of Portugal's rich and beautiful. Today, they are quietly elegant with noble old buildings, beachfront promenades, a bullring and a casino. Cascais is the more enjoyable of the two, not as rich and stuffy, with a cozy touch of fishing village, some great seafood places (the Costa Azul, Rua Sebastio Jose de C. Melo 3) and a younger, less pretentious atmosphere.

Itinerary Options
Three days in Lisbon is a long time for one stop on this tour. If you need a day to add elsewhere, Days 10 and 12 could easily be combined (Alfama in the morning, Sintra, Capo da Roca in the afternoon, dinner and evening in Cascais).

To save another day, Day 13 could be snipped by skipping Evora and taking the overnight train direct from Lisbon to the Algarve (or driving there direct via N120, leaving Lisbon at 4:00 on day 12 and getting to the south coast by 8:00pm).

DAY 13
LISBON—EVORA—INTERIOR—ALGARVE

Getting from Lisbon to the Algarve can be fast and direct, but that's skipping over a big part of Portugal. Today we'll leave Lisbon early, spend the morning and lunch time in historic Evora, and explore the Portugese interior's dusty droves of olive groves and scruffy seas of cork trees on our way to the South coast of any sun worshipper's dreams.

Suggested Schedule

8:00	Leave Lisbon.
10:00	Evora sightseeing.
1:00	Lunch Evora.
2:00	Drive south.
6:00	Arrive Lagos.
7:00	Find private room in Salema on Algarve.

Transportation: Lisbon—Evora (90 miles)
Drive south over Lisbon's bridge on the freeway to Setubal and then east (N10, N4, N114) to Evora. The drive should only take 2 hours.

There are five trains a day (2 hours, change at Casa Branca, from Lisbon's Cais do Sodre station) and 10 buses a day (2½ to 3½ hours) that make the trip.

Without a car, consider skipping Evora, going direct from Lisbon to the Algarve. Trains and buses go several times a day from Evora to the Algarve but take 6 hours and require a change in Beja. Direct from Lisbon to the Algarve, the train takes 6 hours, a possible overnight trip. There are express buses (4–6 hours) that must be booked several hours in advance — get details at the Lisbon tourist office.

Evora
For 2,000 years, Evora has been a cultural oasis in the barren, arid plains of the southern province of Alentejo. With a beautifully untouched provincial atmosphere, a fascinating white-washed old quarter, plenty of museums, a cathedral, and even a Roman temple, Evora stands proud amid groves of cork and olive trees. The major sights crowd closely together at the town's highest point (Roman temple of Diana, early Gothic cathedral, Archbishop's palace and a luxurious pousada in a former monastery). There's a less tangible but still powerful charm contained within the town's medieval wall. Find it by losing yourself in the quiet lanes of the town's far corners.

The tourist info is at Praça do Giraldo #73 (tel. 22671, open 9–7 daily). For budget eating and sleeping look around the central square, Praça do Giraldo. For a splurge, sleep in one of Portugal's most luxurious pousadas, the Convento dos Loios (across from the Roman temple, tel. 23079, $35 doubles). The best food we found is at O Fialho (at Travessa Mascarhenas 14, call 23079 to make a reservation, $10 meals).

Transportation: Evora—Lagos/Salema on the Algarve (150 miles)

After lunch head south, exploring the plains and small towns of the dusty and depressed part of Portugal. The drive is fast and easy if you take the small road from Grandola east to Aljustrel and south to the beaches. The main N120 road is slow and crowded. The Lisbon-Lagos highway is excellent. Expect good roads but more traffic in the Algarve.

Train service from Lisbon to the Algarve (6 hours, four or five a day, overnight ride possible) is pretty good, and it's excellent between major towns along the south coast (nearly hourly between Lagos and the Spanish border). Buses will take you where the trains don't.

The Interior

The villages you'll pass through in southern Alentejo are poor, quiet and, in many cases, dying. Unemployment here is so bad that many locals have left their hometowns for jobs—or hope of jobs—in the big city. This is the land of the "black widows"—women whose husbands have abandoned them to get work in the cities.

Beja, with its Nato base, is nothing special. Its castle has a military museum and a territorial view (open 10-1, 2-6), and the old town is worth a look and a cup of coffee.

A more enjoyable stop on your drive south would be for a refreshing swim in one of the lonely lakes of the Alentejo desert—for example, Baragem do Maranho or Baragem do Montargil.

Plan on arriving at the resort town of Lagos on the southern coast by 6:00. From here drive west about halfway to Cape Sagres, then turn south down the small road to the small beach town of Salema.

Salema—Accommodations and Food

Skip the hotels and ask in the bar, at the post office or on the beach for "quarto" (Bed and Breakfast). Along the road running left from the village center as you face the beach, you'll find plenty of friendly locals with "rooms to let $3.50." Most houses have decent plumbing and many rooms have a beachfront balcony or view. Few of the locals speak English but that isn't a problem. Campers do fine just sacking out on the beach (free showers nearby), or they can enjoy the fine new campsite just half a mile inland back toward the main road.

I had my breakfast and dinners at the beachfront restaurant where the town's visitors gather each night. Their octopus salad will really grab you.

DAY 14
SALEMA—YOUR ALGARVE HIDEAWAY

Today will be a day of rigorous rest and relaxation on the beaches of Salema and in town.

Suggested Schedule

9:00	Breakfast and relax on the beach.
12:00	Lunch and relax on the beach.
1:00	Relax on the beach, browse around town.
6:00	Keep on relaxing.

The Algarve

The Algarve, Portugal's southern coast, has long been known as "Europe's last undiscovered tourist frontier." That statement, like "military intelligence" and "jumbo shrimp," contradicts itself. The Algarve is well discovered and most of it is going the way of the Spanish Costa del Sol—paved, packed and pretty stressful.

There is one bit of old Algarve magic still glittering quietly in the sun—Salema. At the end of a small road just off the main drag between the big city of Lagos and the rugged "Land's End" of Europe, Cape Sagres, Salema has a couple of hotels, a beachfront restaurant, a handful of leathery fishermen and a few lucky tourists. Its beach is perfect with great body surfing waves.

Give yourself an uninterrupted day of sun-simmered lethargy sandwiched between two romantic evenings. June through September buses connect Lagos and Salema (five a day, less than an hour).

Algarve Coast

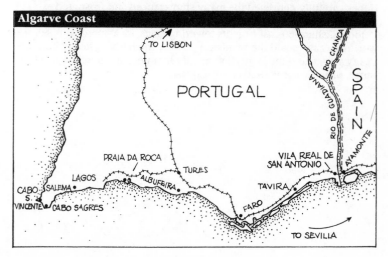

DAY 15
SIDE TRIP TO SAGRES

A short trip in the morning to Cape Sagres, then more free time in Salema and Lagos. It's a tough life.

Suggested Schedule	
8:00	Drive to Cape Sagres.
8:30	Breakfast at Pousada do Infante.
9:30	Explore the cape, the fort and the rugged nearby Cabo de São Vicente.
12:30	Picnic lunch on beach at Beliche.
1:00	Siesta on beach and free afternoon. Options: explore the west coast (Carrapateira is a lovely town), check out the nearest big city resort, Lagos, and the famous Praia da Rocha near Portimao. This beach is the focal point of Algarve tourism. Or, go back to Salema and see how slow you can get your pulse.
8:00	Dinner in Lagos if you want some action, or in Salema if a sunset and fresh fish are enough of a thrill.

Cape Sagres
From Salema it's a short drive or hitch to the rugged and historic southwest tip of Portugal. This was the spot closest to the edge of our flat earth in the days before Columbus. Prince Henry the Navigator, who was determined to broaden Europe's horizons, sent sailors ever farther into the unknown. He had a special navigator's school at Cape Sagres. Henry carefully debriefed the many shipwrecked and frustrated explorers who washed ashore here.

Today fishermen cast from its towering crags, local merchants sell seaworthy sweaters, and the windswept landscape harbors sleepy beaches, a salty village and the lavish Pousada do Infante. For a touch of local elegance, drop by the Pousada for breakfast.

DAY 16
THE DRIVE TO SEVILLA

After several days of storing up solar energy, it's time to hit the road again to return to Spain, setting up for the night in Sevilla.

Suggested Schedule	
8:00	Breakfast and hit the road, driving east toward Spain.
10:00	Coffee break and a wander through the super touristy but still nice resort town of Albufeira.
11:00	Drive further east.
1:00	Lunch in Tavira.
3:30	Catch ferry in Vila Real to Spain.
6:00	Arrive in Sevilla.

Transportation: Algarve—Sevilla (150 miles)
Drive east along the Algarve to Vila Real, where you catch the inexpensive 10–20 minute ferry across the river to Spain. It leaves every thirty minutes from 8:00am to 10:30pm, May-Oct, and 8:00am to 7:30pm in the off season. Despite the frequency of ferries, cars can be backed up several hours. Once across the river to Ayamonte, there's a great highway straight into Sevilla (50 miles).

The town of Vila Real has plenty of rooms, good people watching, and Saturday night bullfights, but is nothing special. Nearby Tavira is a better place if you want one last night in Portugal.

Buses and trains go almost hourly connecting most towns along the south coast from Sagres to Vila Real, where you catch the ferry to Ayamonte, Spain. From Ayamonte, the Spanish border town, catch a bus or train. By bus it's a pain. Three a day (10, 2, and 6:00) to Huelva where a train takes you to Sevilla. Consider hitching a ride from the ferry traffic instead. Remember, you lose an hour when you cross into Spain, so set your watch ahead.

Sevilla—Orientation
For the tourist, this large city is small. Think of things relative to the river and the cathedral—which is as central as you can get. The major sights surround the cathedral. The central boulevard, Ave. de la Constitución (tourist info, banks, post office, etc.) zips right by the cathedral to the Plaza Nueva (shopping district), and nearly everything is within easy walking distance.

By car, follow signs to "centro ciudad." During July and August don't park on Paseo de Cristobal Colón ("Columbus" in Spanish)—it is known for splintered windshields. There is a guarded underground garage where you can leave your car safely.

Accommodations
Sevilla has plenty of $8–20 doubles. The best neighborhoods are in the triangle between the Cordoba station, the bull ring, and the Plaza Nueva and in the Santa Cruz neighborhood (lots of hostales and fondas, traffic-

free, great atmosphere). Our favorite budget bet is the Hostal Goya
Tormes (Mateos Gagos 31, tel. 211170), two minutes from the front of the
cathedral, $12–15 doubles, nice courtyard. For a splurge complete with
antiques, old paintings, and four-poster beds, try the Hotel Dona Maria
(Don Remondo 19, Sevilla 4, tel. (954) 22–4990, quiet street next to cathedral, $35 doubles, great value) or Hostal Monreal in Barrio Sta. Cruz,
(Calle Rodrigo Caro 8, tel. 213166, about $11.50 for a double.)

Food
Skip the "tourist menus" in the cathedral/Santa Cruz area. Eat "tapas" in
bars near the river. Try "Jamaíca," (Calle Jamaíca 16 closed Sunday eves.
tel. 611244) for the best Gazpacho you can get in Sevilla! Or cross the
river into the rather seedy Triana district and enjoy either the "Rio
Grand" (shady deck over the river with city view, good food and
service) or the cheaper self-serve "Puerto" (great tapas and a shady river
perch). There are also plenty of colorful tapa bars along the Calle Las
Sierpes (extension of Av. Quiepo north of City Hall)—great for a bar-
hopping dinner. For a splurge dinner try Rincón de Curro (Vírgen de
Lujan 45, tel. (954) 45–0238, closed Sunday, air-conditioned, regional
specialities).

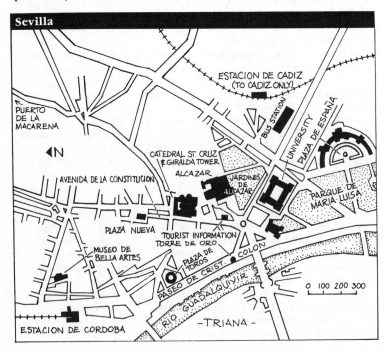

DAY 17
SEVILLA

"Sevilla doesn't have ambience, it *is* ambience." — *James A. Michener*

Suggested Schedule	
8:00	Breakfast—probably in hotel. If not, go local in small bars between Paseo de Cristobal Colón and cathedral.
9:00	Alcazar and garden—beat the crowds, silent beauty.
11:00	Cathedral and Giralda tower. After a cafe con leche across from the cathedral, tour this giant church. Climb the tower. What a view!
1:00	Barrio de Santa Cruz. Stroll through the old Jewish Quarter, peek into private patios, feel the atmosphere.
1:30	Lunch. Head for the river. Too much to eat? Nap it off in the shady Maria Luisa Park. It's siesta anyway and nothing's happening until 3:00 or 3:30.
3:30	Shopping. Get things rolling again. Taxi to the Plaza Nueva, have a cafe con leche and just stroll.
5:00	La Macarena. Take a cab to the Weeping Virgin. Explore behind the altar.
Evening	Relax at the hotel, take a stroll through the Barrio de Santa Cruz and up toward the Plaza Nueva for a nightly people parade. By then it's time to dine. Flamenco is best around midnight.

Sevilla
This is the city of flamenco, Carmen, Don Giovanni, and, of course the Barber of Sevilla. While Granada has the great Alhambra, Sevilla has a soul—one of south Spain's most pleasant cities.

Sevilla boomed when Spain did. She was the gateway to the New World. Explorers like Amerigo Vespucci and Magellan sailed from her great river harbor. Sevilla's Golden Age with New World riches and great local artists (Velázquez, Murillo, Zurbaran) ended with the silting up of the harbor and the crumbling of the Spanish Empire.

Today Sevilla (pop. 680,000) is Spain's fourth largest city and Andalusia's number one city. She buzzes with festivals, life, and color.

Sightseeing Highlights
▲▲**Cathedral**—The third largest church in Europe (after St. Peter's and St. Paul's) was built that way on purpose. When the Catholics ripped down a mosque on the site in 1401 they said, "Let us build a cathedral so huge that anyone who sees it will take us for madmen." Very late Gothic style with some Renaissance. Don't miss the Royal Chapel, Sanctuary, and Columbus' tomb. Open 10:30–1:00, 4:30–6:30.

▲**Giralda Tower**—Formerly a Moorish minaret used to call the Muslims to prayer, it became the cathedral's bell tower after the Reconquista. Notice the beautiful Moorish simplicity as you climb to its top, 100 yards up, for a grand city view. Take advantage of this bird's eye perspective to orient yourself. Open same hours as cathedral.

▲▲**Alcazar**—Much of this Moorish palace was rebuilt by the Christians. The Alcazar is an impressive collection of royal courts, halls, patios, and apartments. The garden is full of tropical flowers, wild cats, cool fountains, and hot tourists. Try to enjoy this in peace at 9:00am. Open 9:00–1:30, 4:30–7:00.

▲▲**Barrio de Santa Cruz (the old Jewish quarter)**—Even if it is a little over-restored, this classy world of lanes too narrow for cars, whitewashed houses with wrought-iron lattice work, and azulejo-covered patios is a great refuge from the summer heat and bustle of Sevilla. Plenty of tourist shops, small hotels, and flamenco bars.

University—Today's university was yesterday's "Fábrica de Tabacos" which employed 10,000 young female cigareras—including Bizet's "Carmen." The second largest building in Spain, after the Escorial. Plenty of student bars and atmosphere between here and the river.

Belas Artes Museum—Sevilla's top collection of art, with 50 Murillos and some Velazquez paintings.

▲**La Macarena Virgin**—This altarpiece statue of the Weeping Virgin—complete with diamond teardrops—leads Sevilla's grand processions. She's so beautiful in her special chapel just off the Puerta Macarena. Take a taxi. Open 9:30–1:00, 5:00–8:00.

Plaza de España—Lovely square, historical blue and white tiles, people watching, and a great park—Maria Luisa—nearby.

April Feria—Sevilla's famous five-day fiesta (usually two weeks after Easter) is exciting, colorful, and very very crowded. Plenty of traditional costumes, flamenco dancing and daily bullfights.

Evenings—Sevilla is a town meant for strolling. The area around the Plaza Nueva and Cuesta del Rosario thrives throughout the evening. For flamenco, your hotel can get you tickets (La Trocha, Ronda de Capuchinos 23, tel. 355028, 9pm-2am; Los Gallos, Olaza de Santa Cruz 11, tel. 216981, 9:30–11:30am and 11:30–2:00am). However, the best flamenco erupts spontaneously in bars throughout the old town. Just follow your ears in the Barrio de Santa Cruz.

Excursion for ruins fans: Italica, Roman site from 200 B.C., 6 miles by bus near Santiponce. 3rd largest Roman amphitheater.

DAY 18
SEVILLA—ANDALUSIAN VILLAGES—RONDA

Today is small Andalusian town day. We'll leave Sevilla early, arrive in
Ronda late and get the best look possible at southern Spain's "Ruta de
Pueblos Blancos"—the route of the white villages.

Suggested Schedule

Armed with a good map, hit the back roads and explore.
Spend the night in a small town, possibly Estepa or the
larger Ronda.

Obviously this Andalusian wander day could easily stretch to two or
three days. The best towns fall roughly within a triangle formed by
Granada, Sevilla and Ronda.

By car you'll hit a good sampling of villages. By bus it'll be slower
going, and the schedules rather than your whim will dictate your plans.
If you're considering hitchhiking, consider renting a mule instead—it's
faster.

Since these towns have very little tourism, accomodations are rather
scarce. Still, a night in a small town is a wonderful experience.

Transportation
This day is really designed for those with a car. The roads are fine, the
traffic is light. Car rental is inexpensive, and public transportation is
sparse. Pick up the "Ruta de Pueblos Blancos" brochure from the Sevilla
tourist info, get a good map, hit the back roads and find that perfect
village.

The Sevilla-Ronda train connection is miserable, but there are three
direct buses a day (3½ hours). The bus station, serving Portugal and Andalusia, is a 5-minute walk from the Alcazar on Plaza de San Sebastian.

Other train connections from Sevilla's Cordoba station are very good.
From the Cordoba station: to Madrid (four a day, 8–10 hours); to Cordoba (two a day, 4½ hours); to Málaga (two a day, 3½ hours). As in
several Spanish train stations, there may be no baggage lockers available
because of bomb threats.

Andalusia
Half the towns I visited were worth remembering. Noteworthy towns
are easy to find so don't worry about missing our favorites. Good information on Andalusia is as rare as it is important—very. There just isn't
much written on the interior. The Michelin guide skips it. Get the best
map you can find (Michelin #446), look for locally printed books as
you're traveling and ask the people you meet for touring suggestions.
Some tourist offices have a handy "Ruta de Pueblos Blancos" brochure.
Here are a few ideas for starters:

Some Favorite Hill Towns
Our favorite Andalusian discovery is **Estepa**. Except for the busy truck

route that skirts the town, peace abounds. Estepa hugs a small hill halfway between Cordoba and Málaga. Its crown is the convent of Santa Clara, worth five stars in any guidebook but found in none. Enjoy the territorial view from the summit, then step into the quiet spiritual perfection of this little-known convent. Just sit in the chapel all alone and feel the beauty soak through your body.

Evening is primetime in Estepa—or any Andalusian town. The promenade or "paseo" begins as everyone gravitates to the central square. Estepa's spotless streets are shined nightly by the feet of ice cream-licking strollers. The whole town strolls—it's like "cruising" without cars. Buy an "ice cream bocadillo" and follow suit. There's a great barber—a real artist—located right on the square. Good chance to make a friend and get a trim.

South of Estepa is hill-capping **Tepa**, where the people go into hysterics when you take their picture. **Menzanares** and **Carratraca** are also stop-worthy. The Michelin guide raves about the Chorro Gorge. Skip it—it's not worth the drive unless you're a real gorge-ophile.

To the north, **Aguilar de la Frontera** and **Puente-Genil** are nice. Aguilar has a pleasant square, outdoor dancing and people who are fascinated by tourists with hairy legs.

A great freeway connects Sevilla and **Jerez de la Frontera**. Jerez, with nearly 200,000 people, is your typical big city mix of industry, garbage and dusty concrete suburbs, but it has one popular claim to touristic fame—it's the home of sherry.

If you're interested, stop at the **Bodega of Pedro Domeca** (Calle San Ildefonso #3, outside of town on the road to Cadiz, tel. 331900, open Mon-Sat 9:30–12:30, closed July). He's the world's biggest producer of sherry and brandy. A free guided tour will show you the whole enchilada including a look at the oldest sherry in the world, 240 years old. After the one-hour tour you're rewarded with several samples to taste.

To return to the cute little towns of this region, drive to **Arcos de la Frontera** (de la Frontera refers to frontier towns from the days when the Christians were pushing the Moors south). Arcos is spectacularly situated on a pinnacle overlooking a vast Andalusian plain. Climb to the church's bell tower—through the tower-keeper's home—for the best view and an ear-shattering thrill at the top of the hour. Driving in Arcos is like threading needles with your car. The Casa del Corregidor parador here is great. (tel. 700460).

Just past Arcos on the road to Ronda (highway C344) is a reservoir in a pine forest with a great beach. A swim here is refreshing, and if you decide to extend your siesta, you'll find a hotel and a good eating place, Meson del Brigadier.

Take the lonesome, quiet and beautiful small road from Arcos to Ronda via El Bosque. Over a pass you'll come to **Grazalema**, another postcard-pretty white town and a fine base for a hike in the Sierra de Grazalema.

Near Ronda are two more white wonders—**Zahara**, with a couple of good budget pensions, and the curiously situated **Setenil**.

As you explore Andalusia on a hot summer day you may see a curious natural phenomenon—the Calina. As the warm air rises, it lifts dust from the bone dry ground. On a windless day, this dust puddle paints the landscape a rusty brown as villages grow hazy and fade into the horizon. The Calina is most common near Ubeda around the headwaters of the Guadalquivir.

Ronda

Ronda is the capital of the "white towns." With 40,000 people it's one of the largest, and since it's within easy day trip range of the "Costa del Turismo," it's very crowded. Still, it has the charm, history and bus and train connections to make it a good stop.

Ronda's main attractions are the gorge it straddles, the oldest bullring in Spain and an interesting old town.

Orientation

Ronda's breathtaking ravine divides the town's labyrinthian Roman/Moorish quarter and its new, more noisy and sprawling Mercadillo quarter. A graceful 18th century bridge connects the two halves. Most things of touristic importance cluster within a few blocks of this bridge—the sights, bullring, view, tourist info, post office and hotels.

The train and bus stations are 15 minutes by foot from the bridge in the new town. The tourist office is on the square next to the bridge. (Open M-F 9:30–2, 5–7, Sat. 9:30–2, tel. 871272).

Accommodations

Places in the Old Quarter are overpriced. There are plenty of inexpensive places in the new town, especially along Calle Sevilla and near the Plaza de España. Try the Huespedes Española just off the Plaza España in the alleyway behind the tourist info office. Choose a place with street noise in mind. The best splurge is the royal Reina Victoria (24 Jerez, tel. 871240) hanging over the gorge at the edge of town. It's a great view— Hemingway loved it—but you'll pay for it ($50 doubles).

Food

Try to avoid the tourist traps. One block from the bullring is the Plaza del Socorro with plenty of cheap tapa bars. Las Canas at #2 Duque de la Victoria (on the corner of the plaza) is small, simple, and serves great food. The Meson Santiago (Marina 3, tel.87–1559) serves local specialities with nice atmosphere.

Side Trip—Pileta Caves

The "Cuevas de la Pileta" are about the best look a tourist can get at prehistoric cave painting. The cave, complete with stalagmites, bones and 25,000-year-old paintings, is 17 miles from Ronda. By car it's an interesting drive: go down C-339, exit toward Benoajan, then follow the signs down the unpaved and dramatic deadend. Or take the train to Benoajan and hike in (90 minutes).

The farmer who lives down the hill leads groups through from 9–2 and from 4–7. If he's not there, the sign says to yell for him. He is a master at hurdling the language barrier, and as you walk the cool kilometer he'll point out lots of black and red drawings (five times as old as the Egyptian pyramids) and some weirdly recognizable natural formations. . . like the Michelin man and a Christmas tree. The famous caves at Altamira are closed, so if you want to see Neolithic paintings, this is a must.

DAY 19
RONDA TO THE COSTA DEL SOL

After a morning stroll through Ronda, we'll make the 40-mile journey from the serenely sublime to the raucously ridiculous: from the un-touristed, whitewashed towns of Andalusia to the hypertouristed, concrete-paved resorts of the exciting Costa del Sol.

Suggested Schedule

8:00	Breakfast.
8:30	Explore Old Ronda, the gorge and bullring.
11:30	Drive 40 miles to the Costa del Sol.
1:00	Lunch and afternoon in resort of your choice: Marbella/Puerto Banus—Home of the rich and beautiful; Fuenjirola—a second rate Spanish Mazatlan; Nerja—Quiet and intimate, by resort standards.
6:00	Experience the tacky but fun Costa del Sol resort scene.

Sightseeing Highlights — Ronda
▲▲**Old Quarter**—East of the bridge, this natural fortress-town has kept much of its Moorish and Renaissance flavor. Don't miss the Casa del Rey Moro ("House of the Moorish King")—built in the 18th Century on Moorish foundations. From its garden, you can hike down an underground stairway—365 steps to the river below—cut by Christian slaves in the 1300s.
▲▲**Ponte de Nueve and The Guadalevin River Gorge**—Enjoy the view from the bridge and the hike into the gorge.
▲**Plaza de Toros**—One of the oldest bullrings in Spain (1785). Ronda is known as the birthplace of modern bullfighting. It's also the home of Pedro Ramero, one of Spain's greatest early matadors (open 9–7).
The "Corrida Goyesca"—A great feria held in early September with plenty of bullfighting, flamenco dancing, traditional costumes, and crowds. (Tickets are tight. Make reservations after Aug 30 at Toros de Ronda, tel. 925–872529.)

Transportation: Ronda—Costa del Sol (40 miles)
By car this can be fast and direct or, if you've yet to quench your hilltown thirst, take the longer but very scenic southern route via Gaucín, Jimena and Castellar. There are three daily 4-hour bus rides from Ronda to Málaga. With no car, if you're short on time, consider skipping the Costa del Sol and going by train straight to Granada.

Along the Costa del Sol, it's smooth and easy by car (great highway across the whole region) and more frustrating by bus or train. The super-developed area between Málaga and Fuengirola is well served by trains (twice an hour, 43 minutes from Málaga to Fuengirola) and buses.

The tiny village of Bobadilla is the unlikely hub of Spain's southern train system. Train travelers, never by choice, always have more than enough time to get to know "Bob." Here are the basic departure times you may be dealing with:

Bobadilla to Málaga: 40 miles, 1 hour
(dep. 10:30, 12:29, 15:15, 20:14).
Bobadilla to Granada: 70 miles, 2 hours
(10:36, 15:20, 20:01).
Bobadilla to Ronda: 40 miles, 80 minutes
(10:41, 11:20, 15:35, 17:13).
Bobadilla to Sevilla: 100 miles, 2½ hours
(15:23, 19:58).
Sevilla to Bobadilla: 2½ hours
(8:05, 12:00, 17:25).
Ronda to Bobadilla: 1¼ hours
(8:53, 10:10, 13:35, 18:16, 23:54).

Costa del Sol

The Costa del Sol is so bad it's interesting. Northern Europeans are sun
worshippers and this is their Mecca. Anything resembling a quaint
fishing village has been bikini-strangled and Nivea-creamed. Oblivious
to the concrete, pollution, ridiculous prices and traffic jams, they lie on
the beach like small game hens on a skewer—cooking, rolling, and
sweating.

Where Europe's most popular beach isn't crowded by highrise hotels,
it's in a freeway chokehold. While wonderfully undeveloped beaches
between Tarifa and Cadiz and east of Alvieria are ignored, lemmings
make the scene where the coastal waters are so polluted that hotels are
required to provide swimming pools. It's a wonderful study in human
nature. For your Costa del Sol experience drive from Marbella to Motril
spending the afternoon and evening at one of the resorts listed here.

San Pedro de Alcantara—A relatively undeveloped sandy beach
popular with young travelers heading for Morocco (good place to find a
partner for a North African adventure). San Pedro's neighbor is Puerto
Banus "where the world casts anchor." This luxurious jet set port complete with casino is a strange mix of Rolls Royces, yuppies, boutiques,
rich Arabs, and budget browsers.

Fuengirola—Torremolinos—This is the most built-up part of the region where those people most determined to be envied settle down. It's
a bizarre world of Scandinavian package tours, flashing lights, pink
flamenco, all night happiness, and multi-lingual menus. My choice for
the Costa del Sol evening is Fuengirola, a Spanish Mazatlan with some
less pretentious older budget hotels a block off the beach. The water
here is clean enough and the night life fun and easy.

Nerja—Somehow Nerja missed the highrise parade and has actually
kept its quiet old world charm. It has a good beach, a fun evening
"paseo," enough nightlife and some worthwhile side trips (the spectacular Nerja caves and two untouristed and lovely villages, Frigiliana
and Maro, are all within 3 miles, served by local buses). Nerja's beach
crowds thin as you walk farther from town. The room situation is tight
in the summer, so arrive early, let the tourist info help you (open 10–2,
6–8:30), or follow a local woman to a casa particular.

DAY 20
GRANADA

"There's nothing crueler than being blind in Granada," they say—
except maybe the stress of being a tourist in the summer heat of
Granada. It is a fascinating city, with a beautiful Sierra Nevada backdrop,
the Alhambra fortress glowing red in the evening and Spain's best-
preserved Moorish quarter. Oh, yes. And piles of tourists.

Suggested Schedule

7:00	Drive from Costa del Sol to Granada.
10:00	Find hotel near Plaza Nueva, park car safely with nothing to tempt a thief in it, buy picnic, and go straight to Alhambra.
10:30	Explore Palace.
1:00	Lunch in Generalife.
2:00	More Alhambra.
4:00	Royal Chapel.
6:00	Explore Albaicin, view from San Nicolas.
8:00	Dinner in Albaicin.
10:00	Do battle in Sacromonte.

Transportation: Costa del Sol—Granada (50 miles)
The quickest way from the coast to Granada is freeway along the coast
to Salobrena and N323 north. But the C335—C340 route via Velez
Málaga through the mountains (2½ hours to Granada) is much more
scenic.
    Trains to Granada (two a day, 3½ hours) have to go back to Bobadilla.
Buses, a much better bet, go eight times a day from Málaga to Granada
in only 2½ hours, stopping in Nerja.

Granada—Orientation
Orient yourself in Granada with the "T" formed by the two main drags
in town, the Gran Vía de Colón and the Reyes Católicos. Nearly everything of interest is near these two streets. Neither the bus nor the train
stations are central, however. (Bus #11, from near the cathedral, goes to
and from both).

Accommodations
Granada has plenty of good budget places to sleep. The little streets
running off of Gran Vía, the area around Plaza Nueva, and the road
leading up to the Alhambra (Cuesta de Gomez) are all good places to
look. For a splurge, the Parador San Francisco, right in the Alhambra, is
Spain's most expensive parador and well worth it. It's a serene palace itself complete with gardens and a view. Call ahead, as its 30 rooms are
often booked up (Recinto de la Alhambra, tel. 221–493, $45 doubles).
For a more reasonable touch of grandeur, follow the signs to the same
parador and book into its neighbor, the Hostal America. Calling ahead

here is absolutely necessary. (Real de la Alhambra, tel. 22747, $20 doubles).

Food
The best places to dine are in the Albaicin quarter—great food, wonderful atmosphere, and inexpensive. For tapas, prowl through the bars around the Plaza del Campo del Príncipe. Chikito (Plaza General Sanjurjo) and El Copo (Martinez la Rosa) serve great tapas. For breakfast have sandwiches, fresh croissants and coffee at Regina Isabel on the corner of Calle de Reyes Católicos and Calle Camelo.

Sightseeing Highlights
▲▲▲Alhambra This last and greatest Moorish palace is one of Europe's great sights, attracting up to 20,000 visitors a day. Nowhere else does the splendor of Moorish civilization shine so brightly.

The Alhambra's greatness is really a symbol of retreat. Granada was a regional capital for centuries before the Christian Reconquista gradually took Cordoba (1236) and Sevilla (1248) leaving Granada to reign as the last Moorish stronghold in Europe. As you tour this grand palace, remember that while Europe slumbered through the Dark Ages, the Moorish magnificence blossomed—fine chiseled stucco, colors galore, scalloped windows framing Granada views, exuberant gardens and water everywhere. Water, so rare and precious in most of Islam, was the purest symbol of life to the Moors. The Alhambra is decorated with water—standing still, running slow and fast, cascading and dripdropping playfully.

Buy a guidebook, use the map on the back of your ticket, climb to the Torre de la Vela (watchtower) for a grand view and orientation.

And don't miss the royal gardens, the Generalife (pronounced: haynay-rahl-EE-fay). This most perfect Arabian garden in Andalusia was the summer home of the Moorish kings and was the closest thing on earth to the Koran's description of Heaven.

To beat the crowds, be at the starting gate at 9:00, skip the Alcazaba, and start out in "la casa real vieja." Most visitors follow the course laid out on the back of their ticket. You'll do the Alcazaba last and enjoy the rest in precious solitude. (Note: this reqires leaving the Costa del Sol at 6:30. Park in the Alhambra lot, and check into your hotel later).

All parts of the Alhambra are open June—Sept, 9–7 and Oct—May, 10–6. Your ticket is good for two days. Ask at the tourist info about evening tours. Consider a picnic in the Generalife. Generalife fountains are often turned off in the afternoon so morning is best.

▲▲Albaicin This is the best old Moorish quarter in Spain. Thousands of colorful corners, flowery patios, shady lanes to soothe the 20th century-mangled visitor. Climb to the San Nicolas church for the best view of the Alhambra—especially at sunset. Go on a photo-safari. Ignore the gypsies.

▲▲Royal Chapel (Capilla Real)—Without a doubt Granada's top Christain sight, this lavish chapel holds the dreams—and bodies—of Queen Isabella and King Ferdinand. Besides the royal tombs you'll find some great Flemish art, a Botticelli painting, the royal jewels, Ferdi-

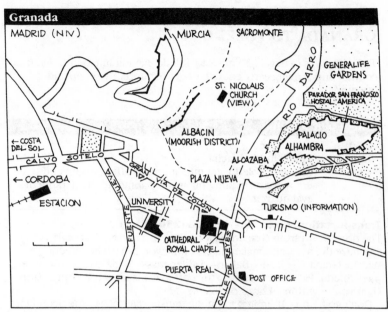

nand's sword, and the most lavish interior money could buy 500 years ago. Because of its speedy completion, the chapel is an unusually harmonious piece of architecture. (M–Sat, 11–1 and 4–7; Sun 11–1).

☹ **Sacromonte**—Europe's most disgusting tourist trap. Sacromonte, famous for its cave-dwelling, foot-stomping, flamenco dancing gypsies is a snake-pit of con artists. You'll be teased, taken and turned away. Venture in only for the curiosity and leave your money in the hotel. Enjoy flamenco in Madrid or Sevilla. Gypsies have gained a reputation (all over Europe) for targeting tourists. Be careful. Even mothers with big eyes and cute babies manage to sneak a hand in your pocket.

Lotería de Ciegos—All over Granada you'll notice blindmen selling lottery tickets with nerve-wracking shouts. This is a form of welfare. The locals never expect to win, it's just sort of a social responsibility to help these people out. The saying goes, *"Dale limosna mujer porque no hay nada que ser ciego en Granada!"* (Give him a dime because there's nothing worse than being blind in Granada).

DAY 21
GRANADA TO TOLEDO

Today's goal is to travel 250 miles to Toledo, having lunch in La Mancha country and arriving early enough to get comfortably set up and oriented.

Suggested Schedule

8:00	Departure.
12:00	Lunch in La Mancha.
4:00	Arrive in Toledo, get info at tourist office, set up and enjoy roast suckling pig in a restaurant in the dark medieval quarter.

Transportation: Granada—Toledo (250 miles)

The drive north from Granada is long, hot and boring. Start early to minimize the heat, and make the best time you can in the direction of Madrid: Granada—Jaen—Bailen—Valdepenas—Manzanares—Consuegra—Toledo. Past Puerto Lapice, turn off to Consuegra for a lunch stop. Then you're within an hour of Toledo.

Don't go by bus. If limited to public transportation take the overnight Granada—Madrid train (23:15–8:00). From Madrid there are 15 trains a day to Toledo, 40 miles to the south.

La Mancha

Nowhere else is Spain so spacious, flat and radically monotonous. Except for the red and yellow carpets of flowers that come with the winter rain, La Mancha is a dusty brown.

This is the home of Cervantes' *Don Quixote*, published in the 17th century after England sank the Armada and the Spanish empire began its decline. Cervantes' star character fights doggedly for good and justice and against the fall of Spain. Ignoring reality, Don Quixote is a hero fighting a hopeless battle, a role by no means limited to people in Spain—or to the past. Stark La Mancha is the perfect stage for this sad and futile fight against reality.

The epitome of Don Quixote country, the town of Consuegra must be the La Mancha Cervantes had in mind. Drive up to the ruined 12th-century castle and string of windmills. It's hot and buggy here, but the powerful view overlooking the village with its sun-bleached light red roofs, some modern concrete reality, and the harsh windy silence make for a profound picnic before driving on to Toledo.

A desert swim? The fourteen deep blue lagoons of Ruidera are 30 miles east of Manzanares at the beautiful headwaters of the Rio Guadino.

Toledo—Orientation

Toledo's street plan is more medievally confusing than any other Spanish city. But it's a small town, with only 50,000 people living in less than one square mile. Because of its present tourist orientation, major sights are well sign-posted and most locals can point you in the right direction if you ask.

If you arrive by car, view the city from many angles along the "Circunvalacion" road across the Tagus Gorge. Drive to the Conde de Orgaz Parador just south of town for a great view of Toledo from the balcony.

By all means spend a night in Toledo. Madrid day-trippers clog the cobbles during the day, but Toledo's medieval moon rises after dark. The tourist office is near the Puerta del Visagra, just outside the north wall. They have maps and accommodations lists. (Open M–F 9:30–2 and 4–6, Sat 9:30–2, tel. 220843.)

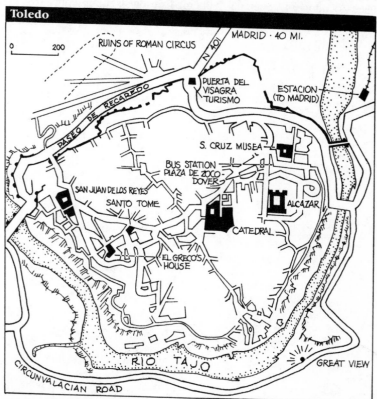

The train station is a good hike from town but easily connected by buses #1, 3, and 5. The bus station, just below the Zocodover square, is much more central. Buses and trains make the 90-minute trip to and from Madrid almost every hour. If you're driving park outside of town in one of the big parking lots.

Accommodations

Toledo sees many more day-trippers than over-nighters, so accommodations are easy to find. Budget places are scattered, though, and it's probably easiest to follow a "hotel runner" to his place from the Plaza de Zocodover. The tourist information has a list of private rooms in town. For a moderate splurge try the Hostal de Cardenal (Paseo del Recaredo 24, tel. 22–4900). It's a 17th-Century palace right at the wall, near Puerta Bisagra. Quiet, lovely garden, great restaurant.

Food

Eating in Toledo isn't cheap. But the town may put you in the mood for an atmospheric splurge. Your hotel receptionist will rarely let you down when you ask for a recommended restaurant. Try roast suckling pig near the cathedral. Toledo's top sweet is Marzipan (try Casa Telesforo on Plaza Zocodover 17, open till 10:00pm). Partridge is supposedly a Toledo delicacy, but every one we've had has been old and rubbery.

DAY 22
TOLEDO—RETURN TO MADRID

Today we tour Toledo, a city of such beauty and historic importance that the entire town was declared a national monument. Finally, we'll complete our 22-day circle through Spain and Portugal by returning to Madrid.

Suggested Schedule	
8:30	Breakfast, check out of hotel.
9:30	Tour cathedral.
12:00	Santo Tome and El Greco's house.
1:30	Lunch and siesta and shopping.
4:00	Santa Cruz museum.
6:00	Return to Madrid, where you have a hotel reserved and paid for from the beginning of your trip.

Toledo
Spain's historic capital is 2,000 years of tangled history—Roman, Visigothic, Moorish, and Christian—crowded onto a high rocky perch surrounded on three sides by the Tagus River. It is so well preserved that the Spanish government has forbidden any modern exteriors. Its rich mix of Jewish, Moorish and Christian heritage combines to make it one of Europe's art capitals.

Toledo was Spain's political capital until 1561, when it reached its limits of growth as defined by the Tagus gorge—and the King moved to the more spacious Madrid. Today, in spite of tremendous touristic crowds, Toledo just takes care of its history and remains much like it was when El Greco called it home, and painted it, 400 years ago. By the way, if you like El Greco, you'll love Toledo. And if you're not into El Greco, you probably will be after a Toledo day.

Sightseeing Highlights
▲▲▲Cathedral—Toledo, Spain's leading Catholic city, the seat of its primate, has a magnificent cathedral. A confusing collage of great Spanish art, it deserves (and we think requires) a guided tour. Hire a private guide. If the $10–12 is beyond your budget, gather a small group to split the price—tell them they need it. The cathedral took over 200 years to build, and under its 300-foot spire you'll find enough Gothic, Renaissance and Baroque art to fill a textbook.

Your guide will show you elaborate wrought ironwork, lavish wood carving, window after colorful window of 500-year-old stained glass, and a sacristy with a collection of paintings that ranks it with Europe's top museums. All the time I felt my guide's national pride saying, "Look at this great stuff! Why do you tourists get so excited about Michelangelo and Leonardo? Take a look at Spain!" It is interesting how little attention we give the art of Spain's Golden Era.

The cathedral's sacristy has over twenty El Grecos, masterpieces by

Goya, Titian, Rubens, Velázquez, Bellini and a carved St. Francis that could change your life. (Open 9:30–1 and 3:30–7.)

▲▲Santa Cruz Museum—A great Renaissance building displaying twenty-two El Grecos and much more in a wonderful setting. (Open 10–2, 4–7 Tues-Sat. Sundays 10–2.)

Alcazar—This huge former imperial residence dominates the Toledo skyline. It's entirely rebuilt, but its Civil War exhibits give the visitor a good look at the horrors of Spain's recent past.

▲Santo Tome—A simple chapel with probably El Greco's most exciting painting. The powerful "Burial of the Count of Orgaz" merges heaven and earth in a way only "The Greek" could. It's so good to see a painting right where the artist put it 400 years ago. Notice the artist's self-portrait looking out at you—sixth figure from the left. (Open Tues-Sat 10:00–1:45, 3:30–6:45, Sun 10:00–1:45.)

El Greco's House—Not really his house, but an interesting look at the interior of a traditionally furnished Renaissance home. Don't miss El Greco's masterful "View of Toledo." (Open same hours as the nearby Santo Tome.)

Born on Crete, trained in Venice and settling in Toledo, El Greco ("The Greek") put all three influences to work in his painting. From his Greek homeland he absorbed the solemn, abstract style of icons. In Venice he learned the bold use of color and dramatic style of the later Renaissance. These styles were then fused in the fires of fanatic Spanish Catholic devotion.

Not bound by the realism so important to his contemporaries, El Greco painted dramatic visions of striking colors and figures with unnatural, elongated bodies as though stretched between heaven and earth. His work is almost as fresh to us today as any current avant-garde artist, so thoroughly "modern" it is in disregarding realism.

Sinagoga del Tránsito—A beautiful part of Toledo's Jewish past. Built in 1366. (Next to El Greco's house on Calle de los Reyes Catolicos. Same hours as El Greco's House.)

Shopping—Toledo probably sells as many souvenirs as any city in Spain. This is the best place to buy old-looking swords, armor, maces, medieval-looking three-legged stools, and other fake antiques. It's also Spain's damascene center, where for centuries, draftsmen have inlaid black steelware with gold, silver, and copper wire.

POST-TOUR OPTIONS

BARCELONA

Our biggest frustration in putting this 22 day plan together was excluding Barcelona. If you're flying into Madrid, it's nearly 400 miles out of your way. By car it's not worth it, but by train it's just an easy overnight ride. Coming to Spain from points north, Barcelona is a great and easy first stop.

This capital of the proud and distinct region of Catalonia bubbles with life in its old Gothic quarter, along its grand boulevards and around its booming harbor. While Barcelona has an exciting past as a Roman colony, Visigothic capital, and, in modern times, a top Mediterranean trading center, it's most enjoyable to throw out the history books and just drift through it. If you're in the mood to surrender to a city's charms—let it be Barcelona.

Orientation

The soul of Barcelona is in its compact core—the Gothic Quarter (Barrio Gótico) and the Ramblas (main boulevard). This is your strolling, shopping, and people watching nucleus.

The city's sights are widely scattered, but with a good map and a willingness to figure out the subway and bus system, it's all manageable. Use one of the three helpful tourist info offices: in the de Francia train station, on the Plaza de San Jaime (in the center of the Barrio Gótico) and at #658 Gran Vía (near the Plaza de Cataluña). They have free maps and accommodations listings.

Barcelona has several train stations. Estación de Francia serves France, Sants-Central serves the south, and the Estación del Norte handles Madrid trains and is also the main bus terminal.

Sightseeing Highlights

▲▲The Ramblas—This is more than a "Champs Elysées." This grand Barcelonian axis goes from rich at the top to rough at the port. You'll find the grand Opera House, richly decorated churches, plenty of prostitutes, pickpockets, con men and artists, elegant cafes, and great shopping. When Hans Christian Andersen saw this street over a hundred years ago, he wrote that there could be no doubt Barcelona was a great city. Don't miss "Mumbru," a fascinating old Colonial import shop (Rambla de Estudio #115).

▲▲Barrio Gótico—Bustling with shops, bars, and nightlife, the Gothic Quarter is packed with 14th and 15th century buildings. Highlights are the great cathedral, the Ayuntamiento (old town hall), several palaces and museums, and the Chocolateria Dulcinea on Carrer de Petrixotl which has been serving delicious chocolate for 160 years—Spanish style (with water), French (with milk) and Swiss (with cream).

Plaza Real—A square worth visiting simply for its beauty.

Gaudi's Buildings—All over town you can find the work of the great Art Nouveau architect, Antoni Gaudi.

▲The Picasso Museum—The greatest collection of Picasso's work we've seen. This is a perfect chance to see his earliest work and understand his genius (open 9:30-1:30, 4-8:30).

Accommodations

There's no shortage of inexpensive places. Look around the Ramblas (Calle Boqueria and Calle Escudelleros are good) or in the Gothic Quarter. The best chance for old world elegance in the Gothic Quarter is the Colon Hotel (Ave. Catedral 7, tel. 3011404, doubles over $35). Our favorite place in a more moderate price range is The Oriente (on the Ramblas #45, tel. 3022558, $25 doubles). And for the best $15 doubles try the Casa del Metge on Calle Tapinería 10, tel. 3101590.

Food

Barcelona, the capital of Catalonian cuisine, offers a tremendous variety of fun places to eat. The harbor area is famous for fish. The best tapa bars are in the Barrio Gótico and around the Picasso Museum. A sort of Spanish Hofbrauhaus—huge and always packed—is Los Caracoles at Escudelleros 14.

Our favorite restaurants for local-style food are: Agut (Calle Gignas 16, huge servings, cheap); Culleertes (Calle Quintana 5, a little better); Siete Puertas (Paseo Isabel II 14, old and traditional, near the port); the Casa Isidre (Calle Flores 12, small, intimate, unknown to tourists); Florian (Bertrand y Serra 20, tel. 2124627, higher class); and Jaume de Provenca (Provenca 88, tel. 2300029, top place for fish, highest quality, reservations necessary).

GALICIA—THE OTHER SPAIN

Galicia, the northwestern corner of the country, is like a Spanish Scotland. The weather is cooler and often misty, the countryside is hillier and green—and you may even hear Galician bagpipes droning across the pastures! You're in "Rias" country now, and everything is different.

Rias are estuaries, like drowned valleys, similar to the fjords of Norway, but wider and not so steep. Most of them are named after the little towns at their shores like Ribadeo, Viveiro, Cedeira Ferrol, etc.

The Rías Altas, between the river Eo and the Ría of La Coruna, are the most spectacular: high, steep cliffs, relatively cold water, often whitecaps, and great deserted beaches. The Rías Gallegas, southwest of La Coruna, are not as wild. Almost like lakes with much warmer water are the Rías Bajas (at Corcubión, Muros y Noiya, Arosa, and Pontevedra). These warm beaches are quite popular, at least in July and August.

This corner of Spain may be underdeveloped, but it's one of the oldest places settled by man: the famous cave of Altamira (near Santillana/Santander) is closed to the public due to deterioration of the paintings, but there are excellent reproductions and original artifacts in the little museum nearby. The cave paintings are 20,000 years old, which is really hard to believe considering how sophisticated they are.

The fertile area here was cultivated and influenced by the Celts, Romans, and Suebs. The Celts left us the ruins, the dolmen and ancient settlements (Citanias). The very impressive relics can be seen at Monte St. Tekla, near Vigo. They also left bagpipes, called Gaita, the national instrument of Galicia. The people are blond and blue-eyed, and more resemble central Europeans than your "typical" Spaniard.

If you drive through the countryside, you'll see more ox-teams pulling carts with massive wooden wheels than any modern gasoline-powered equipment. This may be more pastoral and idyllic, but the paradise has its price: emigration has a long tradition in Galicia. In the villages you'll find a lot of old people, younger women and some children. Adult men who can work go to Barcelona, to the industrial countries of Europe or to South and North America.

Cocina Gallega

Galician cuisine is so good we'll treat it as sightseeing for the tongue. It's an indigenous and solid cuisine, and all the ingredients are of utmost quality. In fact, a lot of the seafood served around the Mediterranean coast originates here.

Lacon con grelos is the national food of the Gallegos, a little heavy (good for the hard working people), but excellent. It consists of boiled pork with a sort of green cabbage grown only in Galicia. Along with that you get potatoes (the best in Europe!) and chorizo, the normal spicy smoked sausage.

Pote Gallego is a stew prepared from the local cabbage, chorizo, bacon, potatoes, beans, and salted pork.

Empanadas are flat, round loaves stuffed with onions, tomatoes, bay, and parsley along with sardines, pork, or beef, sometimes shrimp. Santiago is a good place to find uncountable variations.

For your picnic we recommend a cheese called La Tetilla, and the excellent Galician bread. Both bread and cheese come in the old tried and tested shape (tetilla means teat).

Especially along the coast, stop into one of many Marisquerias, or seafood shops, for lobster, shrimp, crabs, mussels, oysters and so on.

And then the excellent local wines! Ribeiro (red and white) is usually served in earthen cups called cuncas. Watch the red wine, it's tricky! The white Albarinho, similar to some Portuguese whites, is said to be the best of the country. The best Albarinhos grow in Val de Salnes, north of Pontevedra.

The Galicians like to drink their own wines, so it's not always simple to buy a bottle of these wines—often they are not even bottled, but sold only in bars and restaurants. One more reason not to miss supper in one of the many extraordinary Galician restaurants. Don't shy away from the best places. You can eat in Galicia's top restaurants for under $10.

Transportation
The easiest way to include Galicia in the regular 22-day tour is to travel Madrid—Salamanca—Santiago—Portugal. Take the night train from Madrid (21:40–8:18) or from Salamanca, connecting at Medina del Campo just after midnight. Make Santiago de Compostela your home-base in Galicia. Then, from Santiago, hop from town to town south along the Atlantic coast through northern Portugal to Coimbra. There is an overnight Santiago-Lisbon train.

SANTIAGO DE COMPOSTELA

Santiago, once a popular pilgrimage site for all of Europe, is still a beautiful city, and a good homebase for touring Galicia.

Suggested Schedule

8:00	Breakfast in an old quarter bar.
8:30	Browse through the busy market.
9:00	Beat the crowds to the cathedral.
11:00	Tour the Hostal de los Reyes Católicos (info at hotel reception desk).
12:00	Lunch. Have an empanada.
1:00	Try some of the Casa de los Quesos' cheeses.
4:00	See the Museo de Pobo Gallego.
9:00	Dine at Casa Vilas or the Anexo. Be careful, Santiago hotel clerks normally recommend the touristy El Citón or Don Gaiferos. These places are okay but tonight is for real *cocina gallega*.

Santiago de Compostela

Medieval Santiago was *the* holy city of western Europe. Around the year 900, a bright star supposedly led the way to the discovery of the tomb of St. James, one of Jesus' twelve disciples.

This played perfectly into the needs of the Christian Reconquista. Until that time the Moors—strong, united, and inspired by their jihad concept of a holy war—were too much for the Christians. Now the Christians had Santiago (St. James) to counter the relics of Mohammed kept at Cordoba's mosque. The legend spread that Santiago Matamoros (St. James the Moorslayer) had appeared charging through the infidels on his white horse. This tale inspired the Christian forces, and it was just a matter of time before the Moors were gone and Spain was once again Christian.

In the next few centuries, masses of pilgrims swept through central Europe to worship at the church in Santiago containing the remains of St. James. (Santiago is Spanish for "St. James."). 500,000 people a year made the trek, many using what's considered Europe's very first travel guidebook (called *Santiago and Back in 22 Fortnights*, or so we've heard). Twelfth-century accounts speak of the plains of northern Spain being covered with people. Today, Saint James is still buried there, but Santiago is ignored by the modern tourist boom.

Santiago has more than history—it's just plain beautiful. The old center, built completely of granite, shines—especially after a rainstorm—here in Spain's wettest corner. This traffic-free old quarter is a compact mix of monuments, museums, bars, and life.

Orientation

Everything is central: tourist info, bus and train stations, underground car park (Plaza Galicia), hotels, and sights. Outside of St. James' birthday

(July 25—with a great and crowded fiesta from July 15–31) you'll never have to battle the crowds as you would at Spain's other more popular sights. Santiago is an easy town.

Accommodations

In the old town, every other house has a room to rent (lists of private rooms at the tourist info). The best hunting grounds are along Calle del Franco, Rua del Vilar, Rua Nuebe and between Plaza Galicia and the cathedral. The side streets around Plaza Galicia have plenty of hotels.

Food

The places along Calle Franco and Calle de la Reina are good. Drink some Ribeiro out of a *cunca* (white ceramic cup), have some tetilla cheese, almejas (mussels), a delicious empanada (a sort of flaky bread dough pie with meat and vegetables) or pulpo (octopus). The Casa de los Quesos (Calle Bantizados 10, tel. 585085) has a selection of the finest cheeses *de toda la tierra!* Ask the proprietor, Don Waldo Blanco, for his favorites. There's a colorful market every morning between Plaza de San Felix and the Convent of San Augustin (Calle San Roque) for picnic shopping.

For your "Cocina Gallega" experience, eat at Casa Vilas (Calle Rosalia de Castro 88, five minutes from the center, tel. 591000–2170, open 1–4 and 8–12). Josefina Vilas and her two sons are recognized leaders of Cocina Gallega. Be careful, the servings are huge. Nearby, one of her sons runs the Anexo Vilas (Ave. de Villagarcia 21, tel. 598387, closed Monday). It's just as good.

Sightseeing Highlights

▲▲▲**Cathedral**—This huge Romanesque cathedral with its glorious Baroque towers is the focal point of any visit to Santiago. The relics of the apostle are in a crypt behind the altar. Attend a service here, smell the incense, lay your fingers in the grooves worn by millions of fingers over the past thousand years in the Portico de la Gloria pillar near the entrance.

Until the 15th Century, pilgrims slept right in the church. Then Ferdinand and Isabella celebrated their victory at Granada by building the Hostal Reyes Católicos next door. Today it's the town's most elegant hotel ($50 doubles). For those who can't afford the rates, there is at least a very worthwhile guided tour of its lavish interior.

▲**Museo de Pobo Gallego**—Located in the Monasterio de Santo Domingo this museum gives a great look at traditional Galician lifestyle. Check out its fantastically complex 17th century triple stairway. (Open 10–1, 4–7, Sunday 10–1.)

Side Trips from Santiago de Compostela

The Santiago tourist office can suggest a whole list of Galician day trips that you can do on your own or with one of their organized tours. La Coruna, an interesting old harbor town, is just an hour or two away. The Rias coast offers some unique and powerful fjord-type scenery.

THE AZORES

How about dropping in on nine forgotten little islands stranded about halfway between Lisbon and New York?

The Azores are flower pots and aircraft carriers in the ocean. Cows, tea, grapes, pineapples, and 220,000 Azorians all enjoy the mild climate. Hawaii-like volcanoes pop right out of the ocean, creating a paradise for hikers and nature lovers. Three islands are worth a visit: São Miguel, Faial, and Terceira. The others are very quiet and so undeveloped it's hard to find a place to sleep.

Transportation

TWA and Air Portugal offer free stopovers between New York and Lisbon (ask your travel agent for details). Or you can take advantage of cheap round-trip excursion fares from Lisbon (7 to 30 days, $200).

Once you're there, local buses and taxis serve all the islands. It's hard to drive more than 10 miles in any direction without getting wet. A local airline and a mail ship (the Ponta Delgada) connect the islands. If you have time, the ship does the full circuit in a week, stops from a few hours to a day for $60 including a 2-bed cabin without food.

Sightseeing Highlights

Faial—The most international island, nearly every trans-Atlantic sailor docks here. Stay in the 17th-Century harbor fortress, Estalagem Santa Cruz (tel. 23021, $20 doubles). At Porto Pim, a half-mile west of the main town, you'll find a great beach.

São Miguel—The biggest and most beautiful of the Azores, São Miguel (225 square miles, 130,000 people) is a good homebase. It has some fascinating scenery. Don't miss the crater lakes (Lago Verde and Lago Azul) near Sete Citades or the Vale de Furnas with its exotic forests, lakes, hot-springs and geysers.

In the main town, Ponta Delgada, you can sleep in the former American consul's old palace—now the Hotel São Pedro (tel. 22233, $25 doubles, 18th-Century furniture).

Terceira—TWA and TAP flights from Lisbon and New York land on this 15-mile-wide island of 50,000 people. Apart from the large U.S. Air Force base and the pleasant capital town, Terceira is a land of lonesome lakes and volcanoes. Daily flights connect it with the other islands.

MOROCCO

The two-hour ferry ride from southern Spain to Morocco takes you further culturally than the trip all the way from the USA to Spain. Morocco is incredibly rich in cultural thrills per minute and dollar—but you'll pay a price in hassles and headaches. It's a package deal, and for many a great itinerary option.

Don't go to Morocco unless you can plunge deep. Going to just the North coast (Tangiers, Ceuta, Tetuan) to see Morocco is like going to Tijuana to "see" Mexico. It takes a minimum of four or five days to make a worthwhile visit—ideally seven or eight. Plan at least two nights in either Fes or Marrakesh. A trip over the Atlas Mountains gives you an exciting look at Saharan Morocco. If you need a vacation from your vacation, check into one of the idyllic Atlantic beach resorts on the south coast. Above all, get past the northern day-trip-from-Spain fringe.

Suggested Schedule

By Car:

Day 1	Sail as early as possible from Algeciras to Ceuta, drive to Chechaouen. Set up in Hotel Chaouen on main square facing the old town.
Day 2	Drive to Fes. Find hotel. Take orientation tour.
Day 3	Free to explore the Fes medina. Evening classy dinner and cultural show.
Day 4	Drive to Volubilis near Meknes. Tour ancient Roman ruins, possible stop in cities of Moulay-Idriss and Meknes. Drive back to Chechaouen. Same hotel, possibly reserved from day 1.
Day 5	Return to Spain.

By Train and Bus:

Day 1	Sail as early as possible from Algeciras to Tangiers. Catch the 4½ hour train or bus ride to Rabat (Hotel Splendide).
Day 2	Sightsee Rabat—Sale, King's Palace, Royal tomb.
Day 3	Take the train to Casablanca (nothing to stop for), catch the Marrakesh Express from there to the "red city." Get set up near Medina in Marrakesh.
Day 4	Free in Marrakesh.
Day 5	Free in Marrakesh. Night train back to Rabat.
Day 6	Return to Spain.

Orientation (Mental)

Thrills—Morocco *is* culture shock. It makes Spain and Portugal look meek and mild. Friendly people, Arabic language, Islamic faith, ancient cities, a photographer's delight, very cheap, plenty of hotels, surprisingly easy transportation, variety from Swiss-like mountain resorts to fairy-tale mud brick oasis towns to luxuriously natural beaches to bustling desert markets.

Spills—Morocco *is* culture shock. Many are overwhelmed by its intensity, poverty, aggressive beggars, oppressive heat, and slick con men. Most visitors have some intestinal problems (the big "D"). Most women are harrassed on the streets by horny but generally harmless men. Things don't work smoothly. In fact, after Morocco, Spain resembles Sweden for efficiency. The language barrier is a problem since French, not English, is Morocco's second language, and most English-speaking Moroccans the tourist meets are hustlers.

Transportation
Sailing from Spain to Morocco is cheap and easy (two hours, $6/person, $30–40/vehicle, no reservations needed, ten boats a day). No visa or shots are necessary, just bring your passport. If possible, buy a round trip ticket from Spain. We've had departures from Morocco delayed by ticket-buying hassles there. Change money upon arrival only at a bank. (Banks have uniform rates. The black market is dangerous.) Change only what you need and keep the bank receipt to reconvert if necessary. Don't leave the country with Moroccan money.

Those driving cars should sail to Ceuta, a Spanish possession (ten crossings a day from Algeciras). Crossing the border is a bit unnerving since you'll be hustled through several bureaucratic hoops. You'll go through customs, buy Moroccan insurance for your car (cheap and easy) and really feel at the mercy of a bristly bunch of shady-looking people you'd rather not be at the mercy of. Most cars are shepherded through by a guy who will expect a tip. Relax, let him grease those customs wheels. He's worth a tip. As soon as possible, hit the road and drive to Chechaouen—the best first stop for those driving.

Those relying on public transportation should sail to Tangiers. Blast your way through customs, listen to no hustler who tells you there's no way out until tomorrow, and walk from the boat dock over to the train station. From there just set your sights on Rabat. Make Rabat, a dignified European-type town without the hustlers, your get-acquainted stop in Morocco. From there trains will take you farther south.

Moroccan trains are quite good. Second class is cheap and comfortable. There are only two lines: Oujda-Fes-Meknes-Rabat-Casablanca (seven times a day), and Tangier-Rabat-Casablanca-Marrakesh (three trains daily).

Sightseeing Highlights—Moroccan Towns
Chechaouen—The first pleasant town beyond the Tijuana-type north coast. 90 minutes by bus or car from Tetuan. Monday and Thursday are colorful market days. Stay in the classy old Hotel Chaouen on Plaza el-Makhzen. This former Spanish parador faces the old town and offers fine meals and a pleasant refuge from hustlers. Wander deep into the white-washed old town from here.

Marrakesh—Morocco's gateway to the south, this is a desert meeting place that bustles with djelaba-clad Berber tribespeople—a colorful center where the desert, mountain and coastal regions merge.

The new city has the train station, main boulevard (Mohammed V) lined with banks, airline offices, post office, tourist info, and the city's most comfortable hotels.

The old city features the maze-like medina (or market) and the huge Djemaa el-Fna, a square seething with people, usually resembling a 43-ring Moroccan circus. Near this square you'll find hordes of hustlers, plenty of eateries, and cheap hotels. (To check for bugs, step into the dark room first, flip on the lights and count 'em as they flee).

Fes—The religious and artistic center of Morocco, Fes bustles with craftsmen, pilgrims, shoppers, and shops. Like most large Moroccan cities it has a distinct new town (*ville nouvelle*) from the French colonial period and a more exotic old Arabic town where you'll find the medina. Our favorite medina anywhere is in Fes.

Rabat—Morocco's capital and most European city, Rabat is the most comfortable and least stressful place to start your North African experience. You'll find a colorful market (in the old neighboring town of Sale), several great bits of Islamic architecture (Mausoleum of Mohammed V), the King's palace, mellow hustlers, and comfortable hotels (try Hotel Splendide, the Peace Corps' favorite, at 2 Rue du XVIII Juin, near where Ave. Mohammed V hits the medina, tel. 23283).

Itinerary Options

Extend your trip three or four days with an excursion south over the Atlas Mountains. Buses go from Marrakesh to Ouarzazate (short stop), then Tinerhir (great oasis town, comfy hotel, overnight stop). Next day, go to Er Rachidia (formerly Ksar es Souk) and take the overnight bus to Fes.

By car, drive from Fes south to a small mountain town (stay overnight) and then deep into the desert country past Er Rachidia and on to Rissani (market days, Sunday, Tuesday and Thursday). From here you can explore nearby mud brick towns still living in the Middle Ages. Hire a guide to drive past where the road stops, cross country to an oasis village where you can climb a sand dune to watch the sun rise over the vast middle of Africa. Only a sea of sand separates you from Timbuktu.

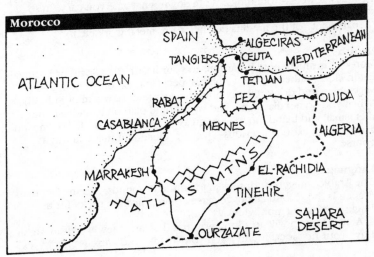

Helpful Hints
Friday is the Muslim day of rest when many shops, etc. close.
Toilets are generally the porcelain-footprint variety. Practice your
deep knee bends (novices use a tripod method with one hand on the
back wall) and carry toilet paper with you.
Hashish (kif) is popular but illegal in Morocco as many Americans in
local jails would love to remind you. Many who sell it cheap make their
profit after you get arrested. Cars and buses are stopped and checked by
police routinely throughout Morocco—especially in the Chechaouen
region, Morocco's kif capital.
Bring good info with you from home or Spain. The *Let's Go: Spain,
Portugal and Morocco* book is indespensible. If you read French the
green Michelin *Morocco* guidebook is also great. Buy the best map you
can find locally—names are always changing and it's helpful to have
towns, roads, etc. down in Arabic.
If driving, never rely on the oncoming driver's skill. Drive very defen-
sively. Night driving is dangerous. Your U.S. license is all you need. Pay a
guard to watch your car overnight.
While Moroccans are some of Africa's wealthiest people, you are still
incredibly rich to them. This imbalance causes predictable problems.
Wear your moneybelt, don't be a sucker to clever local con artists, and
haggle when appropriate—prices skyrocket for tourists.
You'll attract hustlers like flies at every famous tourist sight. They will
lie to you, get you lost, blackmail you, and pester the heck out of you.
Never leave your car or baggage where you can't get back to it without
your "guide." Anything you buy in their company gets them a 20–30%
commission. Normally, locals, shopkeepers, and police will come to
your rescue when the hustler's heat becomes unbearable. We usually
hire young kids as guides, since once you're "taken" the rest leave you
alone.
Navigate the labyrinthian medinas by altitude, gates, and famous
mosques, towers or buildings. Write down what gate you came in so
you can enjoy being lost—temporarily. "Souk" is Arabic for a particular
"department" of the medina (leather, yarn, metal work,etc.).

Health
Morocco is much more hazardous to your health than Spain or Portugal.
Eat in clean, rather expensive places, peel fruit, eat only cooked
vegetables, and drink reliably bottled water (Sidi Harazem or Sidi Ali).
When you do get diarrhea—and you should plan on it—adjust your
diet (small and bland, no milk or grease) or fast for a day. Relax, most diarrhea is not exotic or serious—just an adjustment that will run its
course.

Language
The Arabic squiggle-script, its many difficult sounds, and the fact that
French is the second language make communication tricky for us
English-speaking monoglots.
A little French will go a long way, but do learn a few words in Arabic.
Have your first local friend teach you "thank you," "excuse me," "yes,"

"no", "okay," "hello," "goodbye," "how are you," and "one" through "ten." Listen carefully and write the pronunciations down phonetically. Bring an Arabic phrasebook.

Make a point to learn the local number symbols; they are not like ours (which we call "Arabic"). License plates are numbered with both systems, so you can quiz yourself easily.

Leave aggressive itineraries and split-second timing for Germany. Morocco must be taken on its own terms. In Morocco things go smoothly only *"In Sha Allah"*—if God so wills.

HISTORY

The cultural landscape of present-day Spain and Portugal was shaped
by the various civilizations who conquered and settled on the peninsula. Iberia's warm and sunny weather and fertile soil attracted all early
Mediterranean peoples.

The Greeks came to Cádiz around 1100 B.C., followed by the Romans,
who occupied the country for almost 1000 years until 400 A.D. The
Roman influence carried on long after the Empire crumbled: cultural
values, materials and building techniques, even Roman-style farming
equipment, which was used well into the 19th Century. And, of course,
wine.

Moors

The Moors, North Africans of the Muslim faith who occupied Spain,
had the greatest cultural influence on Spanish and Portugese history.
They arrived on the Rock of Gibraltar in 711 A.D. and moved north. In
the incredibly short time of seven years the Moors completely conquered the peninsula.

They established their power and Muslim culture—but in a soft way.
Non-Muslims were tolerated and often rose to positions of wealth and
power. Instead of blindly suppressing the natives by force, the Moors
used their superior power and knowledge to develop whatever they
found. For example, they even encouraged the growing of wine although they themselves weren't allowed to drink alcohol for religious
reasons.

The Moors ruled for more than 700 years (711–1492). Throughout
that time, pockets of Christianity remained. Local Christian kings fought
against the Moors whenever they could, whittling away at the Muslim
empire, gaining more and more land. The last Moorish stronghold,
Granada, fell to the Christians in 1492.

The slow process of the "Reconquista" (re-conquest) formed the two
independent states of Portugal and Spain. In 1139 Alfonso Henriques
beat the Moors near present-day Beja, Southern Portugal, and
proclaimed himself king of the area. By 1200 the state of Portugal already had the same borderlines as today—making it the oldest un-
changed state in Europe. The rest of the peninsula was a loosely-knit
collection of smaller kingdoms until 1469, when Fernando II of Aragon
married Isabel of Castilla, uniting the other kingdoms under their rule.

The Golden Age

The expulsion of the Moors set the stage for the rise of Portugal and
Spain as naval powers and colonial superpowers—the Golden Age! The
Spaniards, fueled by the religious fervor of their Reconquista of the
Muslims, were interested in spreading Christianity to the newly discov-
ered New World. Wherever they landed they tried to Christianize the
natives—with the sword, if necessary.

The Portuguese expansion was motivated more by economic con-
cerns. Their excursions overseas were planned, cool, and rational. They
colonized the nearby coasts of Africa first, progressing slowly to Asia
and South America.

Through exploration (and exploitation) of the colonies, tremendous amounts of gold came into each country. Art and courtly life developed fast in this Golden Age. Aristocracy and clergy were swimming in money.

In Portugal the fairy-tale architecture of the Manueline style developed. In Spain, El Escorial is a monument of power—anyone building such a monstrous building must have believed his power to be eternal.

Slow Decline

The fast money from the colonies kept them from seeing the dangers at home. Great Britain and the Netherlands also were becoming naval powers, defeating the Spanish Armada in 1588. The Portuguese imported everything, didn't grow their own wheat anymore and neglected their fields.

During the centuries when science and technology in all other European countries developed as never before, Spain and Portugal were occupied with their failed colonial politics.

Endless battles, wars of succession, revolutions and counterrevolutions weakened the countries. In this chaos, there was no chance to develop democratic forms of life. Dictators in both countries made the rich richer and kept the masses underprivileged.

During World Wars I and II both countries stayed neutral, uninterested in foreign policy as long as there was quiet in their own states. In the 1930s, Spain suffered a bloody and bitter Civil War between fascist and democratic forces. The fascist dictator Franco prevailed, ruling the country until his death in the 1970s.

Democracy in Spain and Portugal is still young. After an unbloody revolution, Portugal held democratic elections in 1975. Spain, after 41 years of dictatorship, had elections in 1977.

Today, socialists are in power in both countries. They've adopted a policy of balance to save the young democracies and fight problems like unemployment and foreign debts—with moderate success.

History and Art Terms

Alcazaba	*Moorish castle*
Alcazar	*initially a Moorish fortified castle, later a residence*
Ayuntamiento	*town hall*
Azulejo	*blue or colored tiles*
Feria	*fair*
Inquisition	*Religious and civil courts begun in the Middle Ages for trying heretics and sinners. Punishment ranged from prayer to imprisonment, torture and death. An estimated 2,000 heretics were burned at the stake during the reign of one notorious Grand Inquisitor.*
Moros	*Moors. Muslim people from North Africa.*
Moriscos	*Moors converted to Christianity after the victory of the Catholics.*
Mozarabs	*Christians under Moorish rule.*

ART AND ARCHITECTURE

Architecture

The two most fertile periods of architectural innovation in Spain and Portugal were the Moorish occupation and the Golden Age. Otherwise, Spanish architecture follows many of the same trends as the rest of Europe.

The Moors (700–1500) brought Middle-Eastern styles with them, such as the horseshoe arch, minarets, and floor plans designed for mosques. Islam forbids the sculpting or painting of human or animal figures ("graven images"), so artists expressed their creativity with elaborate geometric patterns. The ornate stucco of the Alhambra, the striped arches of Cordoba's mosque, and decorative colored tiles are evidence of the Moorish sense of beauty. Mozarabic and Mudejar styles blended Islamic and Christian elements.

As the Christians slowly reconquered the country, they turned their fervor into stone, building churches in both the heavy, fortress-of-God Romanesque style (Santiago de Compostela), and in the lighter, heaven-reaching, stained-glass Gothic style (Barcelona, Toledo, Sevilla). Gothic was an import from France, trickling into conservative Spain long after it swept through Europe.

The money reaped and raped from Spain's colonies in the Golden Age (1500–1650) spurred new construction. Churches and palaces were built using the solid, geometrical style of the Italian Renaissance (El Escorial) and the more ornamented Baroque. Ornamentation reached unprecedented heights in Spain, culminating in the Plateresque style of stonework, so called because it resembles intricate silver filigree work.

In Portugal, the highly ornamented Baroque style is called Manueline. The Belem monastery in Lisbon is its best example.

After the Golden Age, innovation in both countries died out, and 18th/19th-Century buildings follow predictable European lines.

Spain's major contribution to modern architecture is the Art Nouveau work of Antoni Gaudi early in this century. Many of his "cake-left-out-in-the-rain" buildings, with their asymmetrical designs and sinuous lines, can be found in Barcelona.

Art

The "Big Three" in Spanish painting are El Greco, Velázquez, and Goya.

El Greco (1541–1614) exemplifies the spiritual fervor of so much Spanish art. The drama, the surreal colors, and the intentionally unnatural distortion have the intensity of a religious vision.

Diego Velázquez (1599–1660) went to the opposite extreme. His masterful court portraits are studies in realism and cool detachment from his subjects.

Goya (1746–1828) matched Velázquez's technique, but not his detachment. He let his liberal tendencies shine through in unflattering portraits of royalty and in emotional scenes of abuse of power. He unleashed his inner passions in the eerie nightmarish canvases of his last, "dark" stage.

In this century, **Pablo Picasso** (don't miss his mural, *Guernica*), the surrealist **Salvador Dali**, and **Joan Miro** have made their marks.

BULLFIGHTING

The bullfight is as much a ritual as it is a sport, so while no two bull-fights are the same, they unfold along a strict pattern.

The ceremony begins punctually with a parade of participants around the ring. Then the trumpet sounds, the "Gate of Fear" opens, and the leading player—el toro—thunders in. Any pity you may have felt for the poor bull will be reduced by a cool 40% the instant the sunlight hits him. An angry, half-ton animal is an awesome sight even from the cheap seats.

The fight is divided into three acts. The first is designed to size the bull up and wear him down. The matador, with help from his assistants, attracts the bull with the shake of the cape, then directs him past his body, as close as his bravery allows. After a few passes, the picadors enter mounted on horseback to spear the powerful swollen lump of muscle at the back of the bull's neck. This lowers the bull's head and weakens the thrust of his horns.

In the second, the matador's assistants (banderilleros) continue to enrage and weaken the bull. The unarmed banderillero charges the charging bull and, leaping acrobatically across the bull's path, plunges brightly colored barbed sticks into the bull's vital neck muscle.

After a short intermission during which the matador traditionally asks permission to kill the bull and dedicates the kill to someone in the crowd, the final, lethal act begins.

The matador tries to dominate and tire the bull with hypnotic cape-work, then thrusts a sword between the animal's shoulderblades for the kill. A quick kill is not always easy, and the matador may have to make several bloody thrusts before the sword stays in.

Throughout the fight, the crowd shows its approval or impatience. Shouts of "Ole!" or "Torero!" mean they like what they see—whistling or rhythmic hand clapping greets cowardice and incompetence.

After an exceptional fight, the crowd may wave white handkerchiefs to ask that the matador be awarded the bull's ear or tail. A brave bull—though dead—gets a victory lap from the mule team on his way to the slaughterhouse. Then the trumpet sounds, and a new bull enters to face a fresh matador.

For a closer look at bullfighting, read Hemingway's classic *Death in the Afternoon.*

Portuguese bullfighting is different. After an interesting equestrian duel, eight men wrestle the bull without killing him.

SPANISH CUISINE

Spaniards eat to live, not vice versa. Their cuisine is hearty food of the people, in big inexpensive portions.

While not fancy, there is an endless variety of regional specialties. The two most famous Spanish dishes are paella and gazpacho. Paella has a base of saffron-flavored rice as background for whatever the chef wants to mix in—seafood, chicken, peppers, etc. Gazpacho, an Andalusian specialty, is a chilled soup of tomatoes, bread chunks and spices. Garlic and olive oil are found to some degree in many Spanish dishes.

The Spanish eating schedule can be frustrating to the visitor. Because most Spaniards work until 7:30pm, supper (cena) is usually served around 9:00pm, 10:00 or even later. Lunch (comida) is also served late (2–5pm) and is the largest meal of the day. Don't buck this system. No good restaurant will serve meals at American hours.

The only alternative to this late schedule is to eat in tapa bars. Tapas are small portions, like appetizers, of all kinds of foods—seafood, salads, meat-filled pastries, and on and on. You'll find many hungry tourists gulping down dozens of tapas while desperately looking for an open restaurant. Around 9:00 or 10:00 they are totally stuffed and unable to enjoy a great meal in one of the nicely decorated and good restaurants.

The price of a tapa, beer or coffee is cheapest if you eat it standing at the bar or sitting on a bar stool. You'll pay a little more to eat sitting at a table and a lot more sitting at an outdoor table. In the right place, however, a quiet rest over coffee on a flood-lit square is well worth any extra charge.

Still, the cheapest seats can sometimes give you the best show. Sit at the bar and study your bartender. He's an artist.

Since tapa bars are such a fun part of eating in Spain, and they have their own lingo and a rather strange lineup of food, this list will be a handy tool when hunger beckons:

Tapas
aceitunas olives
albondiga meatballs
almeja clams
anguilas eels
bocadillos sandwiches
boquerones anchovies
cachelos the best potatoes you've ever had (even better in Galicia)
calamares squid
cebolla onion
chorizo red paprika sausage
champiñones mushrooms
caldo broth
cocido stew
ensaladilla Russian salad
empanada fish/meat pastry (pie)—Galicia
fabada Austrian stew (with white beans)

gamba   Mediterranean shrimp
gazpacho   cold vegetable soup (often with sardines, esp. in Andalusia).
guisado   goulash or stew
jamón serrano   special kind of ham, in the bars you can see them hanging from the ceiling.
lacón con grelos   Galician stew
langostinos   giant prawns
lenguado   sole
mariscos   shellfish
pisto   vegetable stew
pulpo   octopus
queso   cheese
queso manchego   sheep cheese of the Mancha
salchichón   salami
salchicha   little sausages
sopa   soup
sopa de ajo   garlic soup
sopa de verduras   vegetable soup
ternera   veal
tortilla   omelet, usually with potatoes
tortilla francesa   omelet, the one you're used to

Bebidas—When you're thirsty
cerveza (presión)   beer (draft)
sidra   cider
vino tinto/blanco   red/white wine
zumo de naranja   orange juice
agua   water
agua mineral   mineral water
gasiosa/sin gas   carbonated/without carbonation. (Many visitors start their tour hating the "gas," then gradually fall in love with those tiny bubbles—try it!)

And then there is the dangerous mixture of red wine, sugar, orange juice, lemon juice, brandy and the kitchen sink—"Sangria."

Postres—Desserts
helado   ice cream
tarta   tart, pie
flan   custard
higos   figs
manzana   apple
leche frita   fried egg/mild pudding—that's our favorite!

Comidas Cocidas—Cooked Meals
After the salesman of the French-fry maker came through, this machine became the most important thing in almost every Spanish restaurant. But the Spanish language is evidence that there still must exist other ways of preparing food:
asado   roasted
cocido   boiled
tostado   toasted
estofado   stewed
crudo   raw
ahumado   smoked
al horno   baked
a la plancha   grilled on a hot plate
a la romana   in batter, pasta
en salsa   in sauce

Desayuno—Breakfast
"Churros and chocolate! I suppose if one searched the restaurants of the world one could not find a worse breakfast nor one that tasted better. The churros were so greasy that I needed three paper napkins per churro, but they tasted better than doughnuts. The chocolate was completely indigestible, but much better than coffee. And the great gobs of unrefined sugar were chewy. Any nation that can eat churros and chocolate for breakfast is not required to demonstrate its courage in other ways."—*James Michener,* Iberia
pan   bread
panecillo   roll
mantequilla   butter
miel   honey
mermelada   marmelade
queso   cheese
embutido   sausage
croissant   croissant
café con leche   coffee with milk
café solo   espresso
huevos revueltos   scrambled eggs
huevos fritos   fried eggs

Regional Specialties

The dishes of different regions are as varied as you might expect in a country with such deep-rooted regional tendencies.

Galician cuisine has a cult following, and we are fanatic missionaries of the cult. Lacon con grelos, boiled pork and cabbage, along with potatoes and spices, is the indigenous dish. Fresh fish and shellfish, empanadas (meat pies), vegetables, and fruit taste just as they should.

The French insist that the cuisine gets better as you get closer to the French border, and you can't deny it gets a bit fancier. In the north and central high plains, lamb is a good bet. In brash Catalonia, try zarzuela de mariscos (the "operetta of seafood") or their excellent paella.

Moving south, pork out on roast suckling pig in Toledo or Segovia, and try the fried sardines served like french fries found in Andalusia. Andalusia is also the home of gazpacho and sangria.

If you can't get to all these regions, Madrid—centrally located and cosmopolitan—is an excellent place for a "cook's tour" sampling of regional dishes.

Spanish Wine

We think of Spain as only producing cheap, red table wines, and while they do, they also produce perhaps a greater variety of styles than any country. Each region has its own distinct wine.

In general, the north produces the red table wines. Those of Rioja (near the Basque country) are light and oaky and begin to rival the best table wines of France.

Aperitif and dessert wines (sherry, amontillado, fino) are most popular in the hot south, especially Andalusia.

Catalonia produces sparkling wines and brandies, while the central plains prolifically pump out the hearty vin ordinaire.

Most large bodegas (wineries) are open for a visit, though it's advisable to phone ahead a few days before to make arrangements.

PORTUGUESE CUISINE

Portuguese cuisine is different from Spain's, but probably not any more than Andalusian cuisine is different from Galician. As in Spain, garlic and olive oil are important in many meals, and seafood is at least as prominent.

The Portuguese meal schedule is a bit less cruel, though still unusual for the traveler. Lunch (the big meal) is between noon and 2:00, with supper from 8-10. Perhaps as a result, tapas are not such a big deal. You can eat—and eat well—in restaurants for under $4. Here's a list of some specialities you may want to try:

Sopas—Soups
caldo verde   green vegetable soup
canja   chicken broth
sopa alentejana   soup with olive oil, garlic, bread, and eggs
gazpacho   cold, spicy vegetable soup

Peixes—Fish (cheaper than Portugese meat)
sardinhas assadas   barbecued sardines
linguado   sole
lulas or polvo   octopus
caldeirada   fish soup
peixe espada   sword fish
atum   tuna

Mariscos—Shellfish
ameijoas   mussels (try arroz marisco)
satola or sapateira   big crab
camaroes   shrimp
gambas   prawn

Carnes—Meat (excellent, without hormones)
porco   pork
vitela   veal
vaca   beef
coelho   rabbit
assado   roasted
grelhado   grilled

Bebidas—Drinks
agua   water
café com leite   white coffee
cerveja   beer
fresco   cold, iced
gelo   ice cream, ice cube
sumo de fruta   fruit juice
vinho tinto   red wine

At a Restaurant

pequeno almoço   breakfast
almoço   lunch
conta   the bill
carta   the menu
jantar, ceia   dinner
pimenta; sal   pepper; salt
prato do dia   dish of the day

Portuguese Wine

Portugal is famous for its excellent port wines and dry wines. A refreshing young wine everyone should try is vinho verde. Since much of the best wine is only consumed locally and never really bottled, it's smart to order the always reasonable "vinho da casa" or "vinho de região."

Blanco = white, rosado = rose, tinto = red, seco = dry. The local Aguardente (brandy) is good and cheap. Imported drinks are heavily taxed and very expensive. With such good local varieties, there's really no reason not to drink entirely local.

ACCOMMODATIONS

Spain and Portugal offer about the cheapest rooms in Europe. Most accommodations are government regulated with posted prices.
Throughout Iberia you'll find a good selection of rooms. Generally—except for the most touristed places—reservations are not necessary even in peak season.

While prices are low, street noises are high. Always ask to see your room first—you can check the price posted on the door, consider potential night noise problems, ask for another room and even work the price down. Breakfast and showers can cost extra, and meals may or may not be required. In most towns, the best places to look for rooms are in the old—and most interesting—quarter and near the main church.

Both Spain and Portugal have plenty of youth hostels and campgrounds but we don't recommend them. Hostels are often a headache, campgrounds hot and dusty, and the savings, considering the great bargains on other accommodations, are not worth the trouble. Hotels, pensions, etc. are easy to find, inexpensive, and, when chosen properly, an important part of experiencing the Spanish or Portugese cultures. If you're on a starvation budget or just want to camp or hostel, there is plenty of info available through the National Tourist Office and in appropriate guidebooks.

Classifications

Each country has its handy categories of accommodations. Make a point to learn them.

In Spain, government regulated places have blue-and-white plaques outside their doors clearly marked F, CH, P, HsR, Hs, or H. These are the various categories in ascending order of price and comfort:

Fonda (F) is your basic inn, often with a small bar serving cheap meals. Casas de Huespedes (CH) are guesthouses without bars. Pensiones (P) are like CHs but serve meals. Hostales (Hs) have nothing to do with youth hostals. They are quite comfortable, are rated from one to three stars, and charge $10 to $15 for a double. Hotels (H) are rated with one to five stars and go right up to world class luxury places. Hostal-Residencia (HsR) and Hotel-Residencia (HR) are the same as (Hs) and (H) class with no meals except breakfast.

Any regulated place will have a *libro de reclamaciones* (complaint book). A request for this book will generally solve any problem you have in a jiffy.

Portugal's system starts at the bottom with Pensãoes (one to four stars). These pensions are cheap ($5 to $25 doubles) and are often tasteful, traditional, comfy and family run. Hotels (one to five stars) are more expensive ($7 to $40 doubles). Albergarias are like hotels but without food service.

While these rating systems are handy, they are not perfect. You may find a CH that is cheaper and nicer than an Hs.

Both Spain and Portugal have local bed and breakfast-type accommodations, usually in touristy areas where locals decide to open up a spare room and make a little money on the side. These are called *camas, habitaciones,* or *casas particulares* in Spain, and *quartos* in Portugal. Very cheap, always interesting and usually a good experience.

Spain and Portugal also each have a set of luxurious government sponsored historic inns. These Paradores (Spain) and Pousadas (Portugal) are often renovated castles, palaces and monasteries, many with great views and incredible atmosphere. Always a great value, their prices range from $25 to $50 per double. Pousadas have a reputation for serving fine food while the Paradores are often disappointing in this respect. The Paradores of central and northern Spain are usually better than Mediterranean ones. Reservations are a good idea anytime and are virtually required in the summer. The receptionists usually speak English and are happy to call the next one to make a reservation for you.

There is plenty of info on these places both from the National Tourist Offices and in guidebooks. For information on pousadas, write to ENATUR/Avda. Santa Joana Princesa 10A/Lisbon (tel. 889078). An American company publishes a guide to Pousadas and Paradores: Ballard's Travel Guides/P.O.Box 647/Gig Harbor, WA 98335. If you wish to book a room in advance, you can do it through a New York booking service called Marketing Ahead, tel. (212) 759–5170.

TRANSPORTATION IN SPAIN AND PORTUGAL

Public transportation on the Iberian Peninsula is generally slower, less frequent and less efficient than in northern Europe. The one saving grace is that it's cheaper.

Train fares are figured by the kilometer. Second-class trains charge 33ptas/10km (about $.03 a mile), while first-class charges 50ptas/10km ($.05 a mile). Faster trains (Talgo, Inter-City, Ter, and Expresos) add on a "suplemento." Most overnight trains have couchettes (sleeping berths) that cost about $6. Buy these when you buy your ticket.

A 3-week Eurail Pass costs $330 (first class) and would not pay for itself on this tour—unless you're traveling to Spain from the north. It is a real convenience however not to have to buy tickets as you go. This tour uses lots of buses, and Eurail is worthless on those. Eurail travelers must make reservations for longer rides. It's best to reserve your departing train upon arrival in a town.

The Spanish train company, "RENFE," catagorizes its trains as very slow "Correo" mail trains, pretty slow "Tranvias" and "Semi-Directos," fast "Expreso" and "Rapido" trains, and super luxury "Ter," "Electro," and "Talgo" trains. These get more expensive as they pick up speed, but all are much cheaper than their northern European counterparts.

Portugal doesn't have the same categories as Spain—mostly just slow milk-run trains and an occassional *expresso*.

Since trains in Spain are nearly always late, telephone the stations to confirm departure times. Remember, you may arrive an hour after a

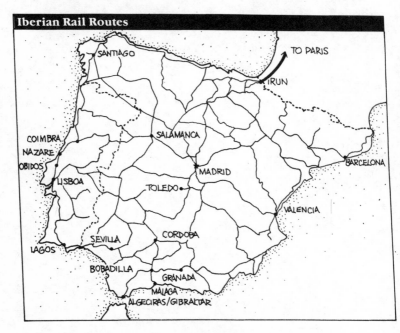

Iberian Rail Routes

train has left—according to the schedule—and still catch it. Use these train station info numbers:

Barcelona—250-4235, or 250-4110
Granada—223119, or 223497
Madrid—222-5998, 222-1961, 222-9328, or 247-0000
Malága—213122 or 214127
Salamanca—212454 or 221224
Sevilla—222693 or 217998
Toledo—221272

For the complete schedule and explanation of the Spanish train system, pick up the "Grandes Relaciones Guía Renfe," available for a dollar at any train station.

Buses will take you where the trains don't—your best bet for small towns. They vary a lot in speed, and are at least as cheap as the trains ($1/20 miles). Remember, public transportation on Sundays and holidays is greatly reduced.

In Portugal, "Paragem" = bus stop. In the countryside, stop buses by waving.

Taxis are very cheap everywhere. Use them, but insist on the meter.

Driving in Iberia is great, although major roads can be clogged by endless caravans of slow moving trucks. Car rental is as cheap as anywhere in Europe—$100/week with unlimited mileage through your USA travel agent or on the spot over there. All you need is your American driver's license. Remember, drive very defensively. If you have an accident, you'll be blamed and are in for a monumental headache. Seat belts are required by law. Gas and diesel prices are controlled and the same everywhere. Diesel is cheaper than gas.

Parking

Choose a parking place carefully and never leave valuables in the car. You'll hear parking attendants constantly warning people, "Nada en el coche!"—Nothing in the car!

Privacy is a rare commodity for the Romeos and Juliets of Spain and Portugal. With so many very crowded apartments, young Iberian lovers can only "borrow the car." Outside of any big city you'll find viewpoints and any romantic parking place clogged with steamy windowed Spanish-made Fiats nearly every night. Not a good place for sightseeing.

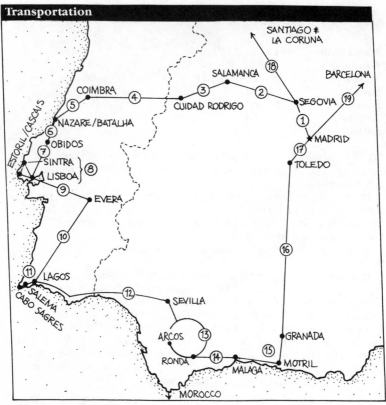

Transportation Segments

1. Madrid—Segovia (50 miles).
2. Segovia—Salamanca (100 miles).
3. Salamanca—Ciudad Rodrigo (60 miles).
4. Ciudad Rodrigo—Coimbra (150 miles).
5. Coimbra—Batalha—Nazare/São Martinho (60 miles).
6. Nazare—Obidos (30 miles).
7. Obidos—Lisbon (30 miles).
8. Excursion: Lisbon—Sintra—Capo da Roca—Cascais—Lisbon (70 miles).
9. Lisbon—Evora (90 miles).
10. Evora—Lagos/Algarve (150 miles).
11. Excursion: Salema—Cape Sagres—Salema (50 miles).
12. Algarve—Sevilla (150 miles).
13. Sevilla—Andalusian towns—Ronda (As many miles as you like).
14. Ronda—Costa del Sol (40 miles).
15. Costa del Sol—Granada (50 miles).
16. Granada—Toledo (250 miles).
17. Toledo—Madrid (40 miles).
18. (Post-Tour Option): Madrid—Galicia (400 miles, 300 by plane).
19. (Post-Tour Option): Madrid—Barcelona (400 miles, 300 by plane).

LANGUAGE

Spanish is one of the Romance languages—from Roman Latin—along with Portuguese, French, and Italian. Knowing any one of these helps with some basic Spanish phrases.

Spanish nouns have gender. There are masculine words, generally ending in 'o' and feminine words ending in 'a' or 'ion.' The adjectives that describe them must change spelling to match these endings.

Pronunciation

You pronounce Spanish pretty much like it's spelled. Don't "cheat" by slipping into standard American sloppiness. *Peseta* should be Pay-SAY-tah, not "Puh-SAY-duh."

Spanish is spoken most clearly with the corners of the mouth tight. This should present no problem if you just smile a lot.

Put stress on the next-to-last syllable for words ending in a vowel, 'n' or 's'. Other words are stressed on the last syllable, unless marked with a special accent mark (like "Málaga").

Pronunciations vary in different regions of Spain. Don't let it throw you when someone pronounces *cinco,* "Theenko."

Vowels

a—as in f*a*ther
e—almost like the "a" in m*a*ke
i and y—as in l*i*ter
o—as in g*o*
u—as in bl*u*e

Consonants

Some letters are different from English pronunciation:
b and v—are interchangeable, kind of halfway between b and v
h—silent
j and (soft) g—like an h
n (with wavy line over it)—like the ni in o*ni*on
r and rr—trilled trippingly over the tongue
qu—like k
ll—like the "y" sound in mi*ll*ion

Portuguese is like Spanish with a French accent. Unfortunately, knowing both Spanish and French would still make it difficult to get by in Portugal. Our advice is to learn a few basic Portuguese words, rely heavily on Spanish (which is widely-understood, though not widely spoken), and try hard to pronounce things like the natives.

As in France, the Portuguese use a soft 'j' (zh-sound) and soft 'ch' (sh-sound), and speak with a nasal accent. For example, the Portuguese *não* (meaning no) should sound like "now" said while holding your nose. (Practice this until you *don't* have to hold your nose when ordering in a fancy restaurant.)

English, French, and especially Spanish are understood by many Portuguese. And, though you may not be anywhere near fluent, the Portuguese will appreciate your efforts to speak their language.

HOURS, SIESTAS AND FIESTAS

Iberia is a land of strange and frustrating schedules.

Generally, shops are open 9-1 and 3-7, longer in touristy places. Banks are open Monday-Friday mornings and sometimes one hour in the afternoon (e.g. 9-11:30 and 2:30-3:30). Restaurants open very late. Museums are generally open Tues-Sun 10-5 and closed Mondays, and many close for lunch. The times listed in this book are for the tourist season. In winter most museums and sights close an hour early.

There are many regional and surprise holidays. Regular nationwide holidays are:

Portugal—Jan 1, Apr 25, May 1, June 10 (national holiday), Aug 15, Oct 5, Nov 1, Dec 1, Dec 8, Dec 25.

Spain—Jan 1, Jan 6, Mar 19, May 1, June 24, June 29, July 18, July 25, Aug 15, Oct 12, Nov 1, Dec 8, Dec 25, Good Friday and Easter (spring), Corpus Christi (early June).

Folk Festivals—Spain

Here are some of the more colorful regional festivals. Most involve religious processions, folk dancing, bullfights (corridas) and fireworks.

March 12-19—Valencia—"Fallas"—carnival, corridas, and burning of colorful effigies.

Week before Lent—Cadíz—carnival festivities, processions.

Holy Week—Cartegena, Cuenca, Granada, Murcia, Sevilla, Valladolid, Zamora—solemn processions everywhere with images of saints. Sevilla's is most impressive.

First week after Easter—Murcia—spring festival

Mid-April—Sevilla—April fair: flamenco, corridas, good times.

During May—Córdoba—decorated patios and flamenco competitions

May 15—Madrid—St. Isidore Festival, a fortnight of festivities.

Whitsun—El Rocio (Huelva)—famous gypsy pilgrimage to the Church of the Virgin. The gypsies come from Huelva and Sevilla along the dusty road either in flower-decorated carts or riding horses saddled and bridled in Andalusian style.

2nd Thursday after Whitsun—Camunas—Corpus Christi: Camunas—mimed mystery play in costume: the struggle of Virtue against Vice: Toledo—solemn procession.

June 21-30—Alicate—St. John festival

June 23-28—Barcelona—days before St. John's festival: night festivities in the Poble espanol.

June 24-29—Segovia—St. John's and Peter's Day festivals with local dancing and costumes.

Late June—Early July—Granada—international music and dance festival.

July 6-14—Pamplona—"Sanfermines": famous corridas and running of the bulls.

July 15-31—Santiago de Compostela—St. James' Festival: processions, fireworks in front of the cathedral.

July 17-31—Valencia—St. James' Festival—battles of flowers and corridas.

August 1-9—Málaga—fair, corridas, etc.
August 4-9—Vitoria—festival of the White Virgin.
August 1-17—Elche—Assumption: Elche Mystery Play
August 14-25—Betanzos—Festival of St. Rock: ancient brotherhood dances.
August 15—La Alberca—Assumption.
August—Corunna, San Sebastián, Gijón, Bilbāo—Semana Grande: sporting events, cultural activities, corridas.
Early September—Jerez—Wine Harvest Festival.
September 24-28—Barcelona—Festival of Our Lady of Mercy: corridas, folk and general festivities.
Week of October 12—Zaragoza—Pilar Festival: Lantern processions, corridas.

Folk Festivals—Portugal

Holy Week—Braga—Holy Week ceremonies, processions.
2nd Sunday after Easter—Louie—Pilgrimage of Our Lady of Pity (3 days), processions.
Early May—Barcelos—Festival of Crosses and pottery fair, dancing.
May 3-4—Sesimbra—Festival of Our Lady of the Wounds (fishermen's festivals going back to the 16th century), processions on May 4.
May 12-13—Fatima—First great annual pilgrimage.
1st Sunday in June—Santarem—National Agricultural Fair, International Folklore Festival.
June 23-24—Braga—King David's procession.
June 23-24—Many cities—general rejoicing.
June 18-30—Oporto—Popular Saints' Festival: the night of the 23rd is a gala occasion.
June 29—Povoa de Varzim—St. Peter's Festival: processions, torchlight tattoo (rusgas), barbecues of grilled sardines.
June 29—Sintra—St. Peter's Craftsmen's Fair.
First fortnight in July (odd years)—Tomar—Tabuleiros Fair.
Early July (even years)—Coimbra—Festival of the Queen Saint: torchlight procession.
1st Saturday and Sunday in July—Vila Franca de Xira—Festival of the Red Waistcoats and running of bulls.
July 25-August 8—Setubal—St. James' Fair: bullfighting, folk groups.
1st Sunday in August—Guimaraes—St. Walter's Festival: fair, decorated streets, giants' procession, torchlight procession, bullfights, fireworks.
2nd Sunday in August—Portuzelo—Folklore Festival.
2nd Sunday in August—Alcochete—Festival of the Green Hat (Barrete Verde): blessing of the saltworks, bullfights, and bulls running in the streets.
2nd Sunday in August—Serra da Estrela—Festival of Our Lady of the Holy Star.
August 15—Many cities—general festivities.
3rd Sunday in August—Miranda do Douro—Dance of the Pauliteiros with wooden sticks.

Days preceding 3rd Sunday in August—Viana Do Castelo—Pilgrimage of Our Lady of Sorrow (three days).

Last Sunday in August—Braga—Pilgrimage to the Sameiro Sanctuary, procession.

September 1–4—Setubal—grape harvest festival, benediction of the grapes, procession, folk dancing and music, fireworks.

September 6–8—Miranda do Douro—Pilgrimage to Our Lady of Nazo at Povoa, on the night of the 8th, folk dancing and dance of the Pauliteiros.

September 26—Cape Espichel—Festival of Our Lady of the Cape: fishermen's festival dating back to 13th century.

September—Nazare—Festival of Our Lady of Nazareth at Sitio: fair, folk groups, bullfights.

1st Sunday in October—Vila Franca de Xira—fair, bullfights, bull running.

October 12–13—Fatima—second great annual pilgrimage.

November 11–18—Portimao—Great November Fair.

BASIC INFORMATION

Money
The peseta (pta) is the basic monetary unit of Spain, worth less than a penny in U.S. dollars. Figure that 100 ptas is about $.66 U.S. (as of September, '85). There are 100 centimos in a peseta.

The Portuguese escudo($) is approximately the same—100 escudos = $.65 U.S.

National Tourist Offices
Some of the best information for planning your trip is just a postcard away. The National Tourist Office of each country is more than happy to send brochures and info on all aspects of travel in their country. The more specific your request (eg. pousadas, castles, hiking), the better they can help you.

National Tourist Office of Spain: 665 Fifth Ave., New York, NY 10022 (tel. 212/759-8822); 845 N. Michigan Ave., Chicago, IL 60611 (tel. 312/944-0251); 1 Hallidie Plaza, San Francisco, CA 94102 (tel. 415/346-8100); Casa del Hidalgo, Hypolita & St. George, St. Augustine, FL 31084 (tel. 904/829-6460); 4800 The Galleria, Houston, TX 70561 (tel. 713/840-7411). In Canada: 60 Bloor St. W., Toronto, Ontario (tel. 961-3131).

Portuguese National Tourist Office: 548 Fifth Ave., New York, NY 10036 (tel. 212/354-4403).

Moroccan National Tourist Office: 20 East 46th St., New York, NY 10017 (tel. 212/557-2520); 408 S. Michigan Ave., Chicago, IL 60605 (tel. 312/782-3413); 2 Carlton St., Suite 1803, Toronto, Ontario M5B1K2 (tel. 416/598-2208).

Telephone Area Codes
For long distance telephoning from within the country:

Spain

Madrid—1	Málaga—52
Segovia—11	Granada—58
Salamanca—23	Toledo—25
Ciudad Rodrigo—23	Barcelona—3
Sevilla—54	Santiago—81
Ronda—52	

Portugal
Lisbon—1
Nazare—62
Obidos—62
Evora—66

Shopping
Spain's large cities each have a royal department store called El Corte Ingles. Malaga's, the biggest and most famous, is a favorite of the wives of Arabian sheiks. With giant selections of everything from high fashion to gold-plated faucets, these consumer palaces are always worth a look.

Iberian Weather

(1st line, average daily low; 2nd line, ave. daily high; 3rd line, days of no rain)

	J	F	M	A	M	J	J	A	S	O	N	D
Spain												
Madrid	33	35	40	44	50	57	62	62	56	48	40	33
	47	51	57	64	71	80	87	86	77	66	54	48
	22	19	20	21	22	24	28	29	24	23	20	22
Barcelona	42	44	47	51	57	63	69	69	65	58	50	44
	56	57	61	64	71	77	81	82	67	61	62	57
	26	21	24	22	23	25	27	26	23	23	23	25
Málaga	47	48	51	55	60	66	70	72	68	61	53	48
	61	62	64	69	74	80	84	85	81	74	67	62
	25	22	23	25	28	29	31	30	28	27	22	25
Portugal												
Lagos/ Algarve	47	57	50	52	56	60	64	65	62	58	52	48
	61	61	63	67	73	77	83	84	80	73	66	62
	22	19	20	24	27	29	31	31	28	26	22	22
Lisbon	46	47	49	52	56	60	64	65	62	58	52	48
	56	58	61	64	69	75	79	80	76	69	62	57
	22	20	21	23	25	28	30	30	26	24	20	21

ABOUT THE AUTHORS

This book is an international effort. After the success of *Europe in 22 Days*, Rick Steves figured *Spain and Portugal in 22 Days* and *Great Britain in 22 Days* would make logical sequels. Rick has also written *Europe Through the Back Door*, now in its sixth edition (1986, 400 + pages, $9.95, ISBN 0–912528–40–0), *Europe 101: History and Art for Travelers* (co-authored by Gene Openshaw, 1985, 376 pages, $9.95, ISBN 0–912528–42–7), and *Globetrotting* (1985, 240 pages, $7.95, ISBN 0–9605568–4–2).

This book is co-authored by three German travel writers. Michael Muller and Cornelia Stauch recently wrote a traveler's guide to Spain and Wolfgang Abel authored the companion Portugal guide. Their research in writing these German-language travel guides was fundamental in the creation of this book. These three Swabians (Black Forest-region Germans) run "Oase Publications" and have published over twenty travel guidebooks to North America and Europe. (For a catalog of their unique and practical guidebooks—all in German—write to Oase Verlag OHG, P.O. Box 344, 7847 Badenweiler, Germany.)

INDEX

BACK DOOR CATALOG

ALL ITEMS FIELD TESTED, HIGHLY RECOMMENDED, COMPLETELY
GUARANTEED AND DISCOUNTED BELOW RETAIL.

Back Door Combination Ruck Sack / Suitcase $60

At 9" × 21" × 13", this specially designed, sturdy functional bag is maximum
carry-on-the-plane size. (Fits under the seat.) Constructed by Jesse Ltd.
of rugged waterproof nylon Cordura material, with hide-away shoulder
straps, waist belt (for use as a ruck sack) and top and side handles and
a detachable shoulder strap (for toting as a suitcase). Perimeter zippers
allow easy access to the roomy (2200 cu. in.) central compartment. Two
small outside pockets are perfect for maps and other frequently used items.
Two thousand Back Door Travelers took these bags around the world
last year and returned satisfied. Comparable bags cost much more. If
you're looking for maximum "carry-on size" and a suitcase that can be
converted into a back pack, this is your best bet. Available in navy blue,
black, gray, or burgundy.

Money belt $6.00

Required! Ultra-light, sturdy, under-the-pants, nylon pouch just big
enough to carry the essentials comfortably. I'll never travel without one
and I hope you won't either. Beige, nylon zipper, one size fits all,
with instructions.

Sturdy Day Rucksack $8.00

This lightweight, 8" × 16" × 4" blue nylon bag is ideal for day-tripping.
Leave your suitcase in the hotel, on the bus, or at the station, and run
around with this on your back. Folds into its own pocket.

Globetrotting $6.00

by Rick Steves (1985, 250 pp., retail $7.95)

A collection of 60 completely new Back Doors in Europe, Asia and the
Americas. Over 250 fun to read pages laced with practical tips.

Eurail Passes
Send Eurail form with check for the pass and a proposed itinerary and
list of questions. Receive within two weeks train pass and free cassette
tape-recorded evaluation of trip plans by registered mail. Because of this
unique service, Rick Steves sells more train passes than anyone in the
Pacific Northwest.

RICK STEVES BUDGET TRAVEL SEMINARS are taught to groups and
colleges throughout the West Coast. Write for info.

All orders include: rubber universal sink stopper and a one year's
subscription to our quarterly Back Door Travel Newsletter. Sorry, no credit
cards. Send checks to:

"EUROPE THROUGH THE BACK DOOR"

111 4th Ave. N.   Edmonds, WA 98020   tel. (206) 771-8303

John Muir Publications

Europe 101: History, Art and Culture for the Traveler
376 pages, by Rick Steves
Finally, travelers have Europe 101! The first and only travelers guide to Europe's history and art. Full of boiled down, practical information to make your sightseeing more meaningful and enjoyable. Your "passport to culture" in a fun, easy to read manual.

Europe Through the Back Door
1986 Edition, Revised and Expanded, 382 pages, by Rick Steves
The lessons of 15 years of budget European travel packaged into 382 fun to read pages. All the basic skills of budget independent travel, plus 34 special "Back Doors" where you'll find the Europe most tourists miss. Sure to make you a seasoned traveler on your first trip.

Europe in 22 Days
Great Britain in 22 Days
Spain & Portugal in 22 Days
Rick Steves' 22 Day series presents travel itineraries for the best three weeks each region has to offer. Each book supplies all the essential information you'll need, including city maps, train schedules, favorite bistros and small hotels, weather charts, a list of festivals, foreign phrases, and even a thumbnail sketch of the culture and history of the region.

Every day is treated as a separate unit and has a suggested schedule, sight-seeing, budget accommodations with addresses and telephone numbers and transportation notes.

And for travelers with less than three weeks to spend, the tour is designed so that you can start or stop at any point along the route.

Quantity	Title	Each	Total
	Europe Through the Back Door—*Steves*	$9.95	
	Europe 101: History, Art & Culture for Travelers—*Steves*	$9.95	
	Europe in 22 Days—*Steves*	$4.95	
	Complete Guide to Bed & Breakfasts, Inns & Guesthouses in the U.S. & Canada—*Lanier*	$11.95	
	The People's Guide to Mexico (Revised)—*Franz*	$10.95	
	The People's Guide to Camping in Mexico—*Franz*	$10.00	
	The On & Off the Road Cookbook—*Franz & Havens*	$8.50	
		Subtotal	$
		Shipping	$1.50
		Total Enclosed	$

Send order to:

John Muir Publications
P.O. Box 613
Santa Fe, NM 87504